First published 2025 by Walker Books Ltd
87 Vauxhall Walk, London SE11 5HJ

2 4 6 8 10 9 7 5 3

Text © 2025 Greg Jenner
Illustrations © 2025 Rikin Parekh

The right of Greg Jenner and Rikin Parekh to be identified as author
and illustrator respectively of this work has been asserted in accordance
with the Copyright, Designs and Patents Act 1988

EU Authorized Representative: HackettFlynn Ltd, 36 Cloch Choirneal,
Balrothery, Co. Dublin, K32 C942, Ireland. EU@walkerpublishinggroup.com

This book has been typeset in Adobe Garamond Pro

Printed by CPI Group (UK) Ltd, Croydon, CR0 4YY

All rights reserved. No part of this book may be reproduced, transmitted
or stored in an information retrieval system in any form or by any means,
graphic, electronic or mechanical, including photocopying, taping and
recording, without prior written permission from the publisher.

British Library Cataloguing in Publication Data: a catalogue
record for this book is available from the British Library

ISBN 978-1-5295-2249-5

www.walker.co.uk

TOTALLY CHAOTIC HISTORY
THE STONE AGE RUNS WILD!

GREG JENNER
with Dr BRENNA HASSETT
illustrated by RIKIN PAREKH

WALKER BOOKS

For Esmé, the best little human
since *Homo floresiensis*!
G.J.

For all those *sapiens* whose
work got us this far.
B.H.

WELCOME TO THE STONE AGE!

So you're curious about the Stone Age, huh? You fancy hanging out in a cave, wrestling a sabretooth tiger and hunting a mammoth for your dinner? Well, you've chosen the right book – congrats! You'll find out everything you ever wanted to know about what life was like hundreds of thousands of years ago. But don't expect a dry textbook droning on about dusty old facts, because this book is actually about …

(… and also the Stone Age)

Hello! I'm Greg. I'm a public historian, which means my job is making history fun for everyone. In this book, I'm going to take you on the most ludicrously chaotic journey in human history ... because it's *literally* the story of how we became human in the first place! It's a totally weird and wild story that squishes 34 million years into one short book, so hold on tight!

As we're zooming along, watch out for my trusty chaos meter. It will tell you whether things are looking pretty chill, or if we're about to hit a spell of TOTAL CHAOS!

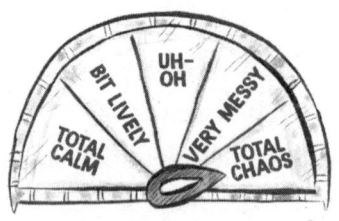

Oh, and we won't do this journey alone. You see, historians like me study only the last 5,000 years (the period after the invention of writing) – that's HISTORY! – but this story is actually *pre*history. So I need an expert to help *me* to help *you*! Please meet the brilliantly brainy Dr Brenna Hassett: she's an archaeologist – which means she digs up evidence of the past – and she studies ancient bones, which also makes her a biological anthropologist.

That's me!

Brenna will be popping up with her accuracy alarm to put us right whenever I say something too silly! Or if there's a brand-new discovery that we need to know about. Amazingly, archaeological discoveries happen all the time and can massively change our understanding of the Stone Age!

BEEEEEEEP!

I'll also scribble in the margins, like this!

Even facts in this book will get overturned – that's the fun challenge of studying the Stone Age!

WHAT HAPPENS NEXT?!

Maybe you've always thought history is just a set of dates and facts to learn – but it's so much more exciting than that. What if you imagined what it was like to actually live through the Stone Age? Remember, nobody in the Stone Age knew what was coming next – they couldn't know if tomorrow might bring an Ice Age, or an extinction, or an intergalactic alien teaching them how to boogie! The Stone Age was wildly unpredictable, and that's exactly what you're going to experience in this book!

This absolutely did not happen, Greg!

So grab on to something tightly, because we're about to hurtle at record speed through 7 million years of human evolution!

SO YOU THINK YOU KNOW THE STONE AGE?

OK, we'll begin with an easy question – what do you imagine when I say Stone Age? Maybe something like this…

Yeah, some of these are correct... But dinosaurs? NO WAY! They died out about 63 million years before the Stone Age began, so they're banned from this book. GET OUT, DINOS, YOU'RE NOT WELCOME HERE!

However, even though the other stuff is correct, the story of the Stone Age is waaaaaaaay messier than you'd think, and there's loads more myths to bust. For example, did you know that...

- *Some people in the Stone Age were cannibals!*
- *Neanderthals had bigger brains than us.*
- *There was a Stone Age bird in Australia nicknamed the Demon Duck of Doom!*
- *Exciting new developments didn't happen everywhere at once. Prehistoric Britain was often way behind what was going on elsewhere!*

Surprising, right? But before we begin our roller coaster ride through several million years, let's have a cheeky glimpse at a timeline, so you know what to expect...

Scientists don't call the Stone Age "the Stone Age" — they split it up into different sections called eras.

TIMELINE OF

BEFORE THE STONE AGE

34 million years ago
All humans are descended from something like a tree shrew — this is the earliest one we know about!

7 million years ago
The earliest known hominins (the scientific name for humans and their ancestors) live in Africa.

LOWER PALAEOLITHIC

3.3 million years ago
Hominins first start making tools to help them process their food.

1.8 million years ago
Homo erectus a the first huma ancestors to lea Africa and go ir Europe, the Mid East and Asia

15,000–30,000 years ago
Humans breed dogs.

23,000 years ago
Humans start grinding up grasses and experimenting with living in the same place all year round.

25,000 years ago
Humans reach North America across the Bering Strait land bridge.

40,000 years ago
Neanderthals go extinct, leaving only Homo sapiens.

50,000 years ago
Three hominin species go extinct, leaving only Homo sapiens and Neanderthals.

UPPER PALAEOLITHIC

MESOLITHIC/NEOLITHIC

11,700 years ago
The climate changes and ends an Ice Age in Europe and North America.

11,000 years ago
The first big stone temple, Göbekli Tepe, is built in modern Türkiye.

11,000 years ago
Humans work out how to farm crops and create new species of domesticated animals.

10,000 years ago
Lots of big animals in North America go extinct.

9,500 years ago
One of the first villages ever is in Çatalhöyük, Türkiye.

THE STONE AGE

MIDDLE PALAEOLITHIC

780,000 years ago
Hominins discover fire – and then cooking!

500,000 years ago
The muddle in the middle! Lots of new hominin species appear all over the place!

400,000 years ago
Neanderthals (*Homo neanderthalensis*) evolve in Europe.

300,000 years ago
Homo sapiens (humans) evolve in Africa.

110,000 years ago
Homo erectus go extinct. They are the most successful hominin species of all time, surviving for almost 2 million years!

90,000 years ago
Homo sapiens manage to leave Africa and start living elsewhere (after a couple of failed attempts).

65,000 years ago
Homo sapiens reach Australia and start living there.

51,000 years ago
Homo sapiens start to paint animals on cave walls.

NEOLITHIC

6,500 years ago
European farmers arrive in Britain and wipe out 99% of the population!

5,000 years ago
People build stone houses in Skara Brae, Orkney.

5,000 years ago
Stonehenge is built as part of a group of ritual monuments in Britain.

4,600 years ago
End of the Stone Age; start of the Bronze Age!

Hominin is the scientific group that includes humans and their prehistoric ancestors.

As you can see, the Stone Age isn't JUST the Stone Age. It's millions of years, split up into chunks, during which there were loads of different species of hominins appearing, dying out, exploring new lands, inventing new technologies and experimenting with new ways to live.

Think you can handle the chaos? Then let's swing into action!

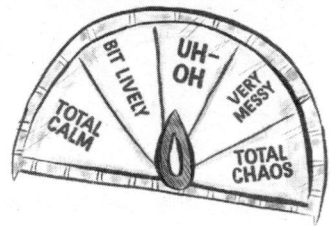

2
OUT OF THE TREES

We're pre-Palaeolithic – that means before the Stone Age!

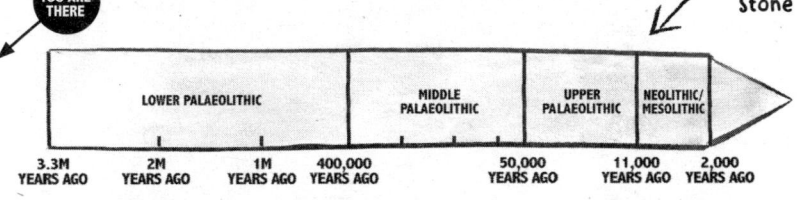

You are a human – congratulations, that's a pretty cool thing to be. But where do you think our human story starts? A hundred thousand years ago? Five million years ago? Last Tuesday? Well, we could begin in loads of places, but in order to understand how we ended up with early humans running around chasing mammoths, we need to know what comes BEFORE the Stone Age. So let's begin up a tree, right in the middle of East Asia, a whopping 34 million years ago. This is the start of our human journey.

Humans are pretty new, but we're not THAT new!

And what incredible tree-dwelling creature are we encountering? A cheeky little monkey? A powerful gorilla? A fully grown businesswoman in a snazzy shirt and skirt? Nope! Let me introduce you to your very, very, very, very-multiplied-by-a-million distant cousin: *Ptilocercus kylin*, otherwise known as a ...

TREE SHREW!

Aww, sooooooo cute!

Amazingly, something like this dinky creature – with its mouselike body and long ratty tail – will gradually evolve into us: HUMANS! But it's going to take 34 million years, and the journey is going to be VERY chaotic. In fact, the first thing to explain is what I even mean by "evolve". Basically, it's when a radioactive spider bites a teenager and they evolve mutant superpowers—

Modern tree shrews are sometimes nicknamed "living fossils" because they have barely evolved in 34 million years!

EVOLUTION

No, Greg! Evolution is when species naturally change over time due to random copying mistakes made when they have babies (reproduce). These genetic mistakes, or mutations, get passed down through the generations, particularly when they're useful. So if a rabbit species evolved longer legs, it could outrun hungry foxes, allowing it to live longer and have more babies.

All of this is pure random luck – you can't choose when to evolve, or with what new skill. It's not like a power-up in a video game. Evolution is pure chaos! It's often dubbed the "survival of the fittest", but "fittest" doesn't mean sportiest – it means the best *suited* to the natural environment. Evolution can take millions of years, or happen within just a few generations. But, if the changes keep piling up, eventually you end up with a totally new species – like how dolphins evolved from a sort of wolf-camel-hippo mix that lived on land!

FROM SHREWS TO CHIMPS

Ah, gotcha! Right, where were we? Oh yeah, the adorable tree shrew from 34 million years ago! Well, it's very cute, but it's not what we came here for, is it? Nah, we need something more ... uh ... human-shaped. And if evolution can take millions of years, I'm not hanging around for all that time. Let's just watch the highlights reel!

HIGHLIGHTS REEL

Africa, nearly 10 million years ago.

Tree shrews have evolved into much larger tree-dwelling, fruit-gobbling apes.

Then ... heatwave!

Forests shrink back in the heat.

The apes are forced down to the ground to scrabble around for grasses, seeds and nuts to munch.

These are tougher than fruits, so their teeth evolve to grind, chomp and chew.

These apes still swing through the trees with their chimp-like hands and flexible shoulders.

7 million years ago. Africa's climate keeps changing, which means... MORE EVOLUTION!

These new apes are walking upright on two legs!

WHOAAAAAAAAAAAAAAA!!!

They're walking around on two legs, just like I do! So, with this creature starting to look a bit human-ish, I'm sure it won't be long until the weather changes again, and we get to meet modern humans like you and me, and— Er, HANG ON – WHO IS THIS??!!

Another hominin species just emerged out of nowhere! Right … uh … well, I guess let's wave hello to—

Sahelanthropus tchadensis

WAIT, there's another one!

Orrorin tugenensis

Ardipithecus

And ANOTHER!

What is happening?! Who are these little guys, and why do they have big toes that stick out and move like foot thumbs? Is it to help them climb trees? I thought hominins were coming *down* from the trees?

Evolution is not that straightforward...

CHAOTIC EVOLUTION!

Oh dear, we've barely started the book and already things are chaotic! Because major climate change keeps happening every 200,000 years, these early African hominins keep splintering off into many new species.

And it's not even the case that each new species looks more and more like us. Actually, although they all have stuff in common, they have loads of differences! Some have wrists and feet designed for tree-climbing; some have smaller teeth; some walk upright; some still use all four limbs; some have tiny brains; others have larger noggins… It's quite hard to keep track! Let's keep it simple. Us modern-day humans are known by the fancy sciencey name *Homo sapiens*. So, Brenna, which of these early hominins is the ancestor of *Homo sapiens*? That's the only one I care about!

Like those sticky-out foot thumbs!

Tree climbing? That's so last year!

ACCURACY ALARM

WHO DO YOU THINK YOU WERE?

Sorry, Greg, it's incredibly tricky figuring this out! Between 7 million and 2 million years ago, there were over twenty different hominin species that might have been our ancestors! A new theory says climate change meant Africa's environment kept changing, forcing hominins to keep swapping between grassy savannahs, leafy woodlands and thick forests. This left our ancestors with a lot of adapting to do and could explain why there were SO MANY different species! Untangling human evolution is chaotic and confusing, and we're still working out the family tree. We even used to think a species called *Gigantopithecus blacki* was related to us, but then we realized it's not even human – it was just a massive orang-utan!

Uh ... thanks, Brenna, I'm definitely not confused. Not at all. Um... Look, can we just keep moving forward? Because something very cool is happening: these hominins are starting to make and use tools! This is so exciting; it actually officially marks the start of the Stone Age. So, I think we'd better find out more about it, yeah?

TOOL TIME!

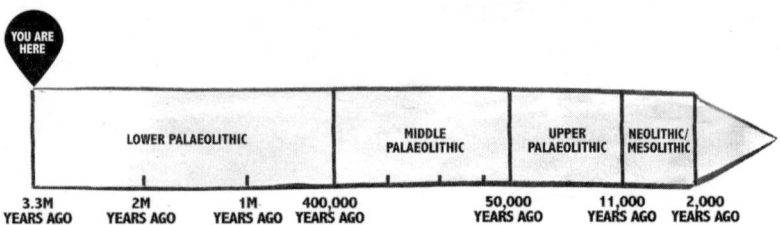

To recap, there are loads of different hominins running around Africa, and we're probably distantly related to some of them, and now they're starting to get good at toolmaking, and they're using these stone tools to slice up dead animal carcasses left by other predators…

Hunting was invented much later!

That's the proper name for the earliest Stone Age era!

Oh, sorry, were you expecting the early Stone Age to be a time of hunting? Nope! Here in the Lower Palaeolithic era, it's all about scavenging – that's when you let the big scary lions and other predators do all the hard work, and then eat their leftovers! And the hominins' simple stone tools allow them to cut up the animal meat, smash open bones and devour the tasty marrow inside! This is super useful and—

CALLING ALL HOMININS!

Wanna cut your animal flesh faster?

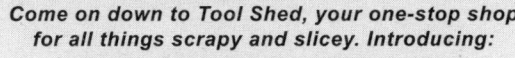

Come on down to Tool Shed, your one-stop shop for all things scrapy and slicey. Introducing:
THE SHARP-EDGED SMASHER
This fantastic multi-tool can do it all: slicing, smashing *and* scraping! We've perfected the design of the first EVER stone tools.

GET YOURS TODAY!

HEY! I NEVER SAID THIS BOOK COULD HAVE ADVERTS!!! What's going on? Although, that ad is correct – these sharp-edged smashers are the first tools hominins make out of rocks to scavenge food.

And hominins are getting better at toolmaking. If we jump forward a few hundred thousand years we find—

NEW FOR 2.6 MILLION YEARS AGO!

IMPROVED SHARP-EDGED SMASHER
Crafted by holding both stones in our hands and bashing them together, resulting in a higher-quality finish. Upgrade now!

AARGH! I hate pop-up ads, they're so annoying! Anyway, let's find out more about how hominins make these tools. All you need is a big knap session. No, I don't mean a mid-afternoon snooze!

These very earliest stone tools are called Lomekwian, named after where they were found in Kenya, Africa.

LET'S GET KNAPPY HAPPY!

Knapping (the "K" is silent) is how you make a tool from a rock. Sure, chimps can bash stuff with a round rock, but only hominins know how to sharpen and shape the rock's edges into something much cleverer and more effective.

To make the simplest tool, they take a nice hard rock with a smooth inside and bang it against an anvil stone on the ground to gradually chip little flakes off one side, creating a slicing edge – careful with your fingers!

To make a more complex tool, or even a double-edged cutter, they grab a rock in each hand and carefully bang them together. Sometimes tiny sharp flakes fly off, which can be useful too.

These early stone tools are all that hominins have to work with, and they're pretty effective, but it's not what comes to mind when I think of *tools*… Where are the power drills and screwdrivers?!

ACCURACY ALARM

BEEEEEEEP! BEEEEEEEP!

TOOLS ROCK!

That's a long way off! We're used to fancy modern technology, but a tool is anything you can craft or change to do a particular job. The first ever hominin to create new tools was probably *Kenyanthropus platyops* (which means "flat-faced Kenya man"), who lived 3.3 million years ago in East Africa. Their Lomekwian tools were very simple. Next came Oldowan tools, roughly 2.6 million years ago, and they were used in Africa, Europe and South and East Asia for a very long time.

MEET YOUR ANCESTOR!

Someone super important is using these super-handy new tools: there's a new hominin in town and – FANFARE, PLEASE! – they are the first species that we can say is DEFINITELY a human ancestor! Hello, *Homo habilis*!

HOMO HABILIS
NEW SPECIES

HOMO WHO-BILIS?

Sorry to interrupt again, Greg! You're right, *Homo habilis* are probably our ancestor. Their name means "handy man" and they were called this because in the 1960s, scientists thought they were the first hominin species to use tools. However, we now know tools were being used by an earlier species. But it seems really mean to strip *habilis* of their cute nickname, so they can stay *Homo habilis* for now!

OK, so even if their name is slightly misleading, *Homo habilis* are still important – and I for one am happy to finally meet a human ancestor.

But you know the saying that you can wait ages for a bus, and then loads all come at once? Well, if we wait a mere few hundred thousand years, we've got another human ancestor! Yep, look who's wandering around the trees over there: they're bigger; they're stronger; they are *Homo erectus*. I think they need their own chapter!

4
ERECTUS GOES WALKABOUT

Honestly, I've already lost count of how many hominin species we've met so far – maybe thirteen? But I think this new one, *Homo erectus*, might be important. After all, they're carrying something pretty snazzy – a new kind of tool we've not seen before tha—

NEW TO TOOL SHED!!!

DOUBLE-EDGED HAND AXE!

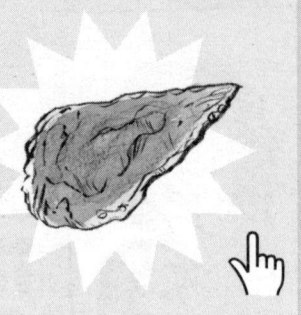

Want the absolute best kit? Don't be a tool fool! Upgrade now to the **DOUBLE-EDGED HAND AXE**. Its pear-shaped design and sharpened edges on both sides gives you **DOUBLE** the slicing power and dexterity. You'll be the envy of all your besties!

These Acheulean tools were first found in Saint-Acheul in France, but were also used in prehistoric Africa and Asia.

AARGH, not another ad! It's true, though. These *Homo erectus* are carrying <u>fancy new hand axes</u> which are multipurpose tools for scraping, slicing, hammering and digging. With technology this good, I think *Homo erectus* have a good chance of sticking around for a while!

ACCURACY ALARM

LONG LIVE HOMO ERECTUS!

BEEEEEEEP! BEEEEEEEP!

That's right – in fact, *Homo erectus* is the most successful human species of all time. They survived on the planet for maybe 1.8 million years, which is waaaaaaay longer than we modern humans have lived for!

Really?! In that case, we'd better find out more about them!

FACT FILE: HOMO ERECTUS

HEIGHT: 1.45–1.65 metres
WEIGHT: 40–65 kilograms
BRAIN SIZE: Quite small.
FAVE FOODS: Nuts, fruit, plants, wild pigs, huge scary wild cows, huge scary wild horses, huge scary wild elephants.
SPECIAL SKILLS: Expert tool users. Very good at walking.

SCAVENGER LIFE

Right, they're not the prettiest to look at, but *Homo erectus* are definitely very good at walking – their hips let them move in a straight line, without swaying side to side like waddling chimps. And they've got some smart ways of scavenging.

In fact— SHH! Keep your voice down! I've just spotted a small family of *erectus* hiding in the grass over there. They have spent days tracking a herd of wild pigs through the African grasslands. One of the pigs was attacked by a predator, which snacked on it and then wandered off, and now a pack of hyenas has shown up to scavenge on the body. The *erectus* family are waiting for the hyenas to finish their meal. Hmm, it's not exactly fast food, but it's definitely safer to wait their turn and—

PROWLING PREDATORS

Oops, sorry, Greg! I forgot to mention all these hominins weren't just roaming the Earth peacefully on their own. Scimitar-toothed cats (*Homotherium*) were brilliant predators that thrived for several million years and only went extinct 30,000 years ago! They were one of the hunters that left scraps behind for hominins to scavenge. They were as big as lions, with powerful jaws that acted like clamps to hold prey still, and long canine teeth shaped like curved scimitar swords. However, *Homotherium* were bad at finishing their meals! Their teeth couldn't break bones, meaning there was lots of meat and marrow left. Cunning *Homo erectus* could sneak in afterwards, with their tools, to finish the job.

YIKES! Is it gone?! These killer kitties hunt in packs, so let's get out of here before we end up as pudding! Those *Homo erectus* are braver than me. I wouldn't want to hang around, risking a fight with dangerous hyenas and terrifying murder cats!

I wonder if our other ancestor, *Homo habilis*, does the same thing? Let's go and check in on them… OH, WHERE DID THEY GO? I can't see them anywhere; they must have gone extinct. What a shame! ← Yep, they died out 1.6 million years ago!

At least *Homo erectus* have avoided dying out. Maybe the extra calories from their meaty meals are helping them to grow bigger brains. If only I could snack myself smarter by eating my favourite crisps!

OUT OF AFRICA

So, *Homo erectus* are doing brilliantly in Africa because they've found a reliable way to get big meals and— WAIT A SEC! Where are the stabby-toothed killer cats going? They're suddenly heading north. I wonder why? Oh, I don't believe it – the African climate is changing yet again! Honestly, you just can't rely on anything around here, can you?

Yes, the forests are shrinking and the savannah grasslands are growing, which is bad news for the big cats who love to hide in thick foliage. They're wandering off in search of more tree cover, which means no more free dinners for *Homo erectus*.

Uh … hang on! Turns out *Homo erectus* are going north with them! These two species are definitely not buddies – the cats would happily rip a hominin's guts out – but maybe *erectus* have decided to follow them wherever they go, dining on kitty cat scraps from a safe distance. This means hominins are about to leave Africa for the very first time!

ON THE MOVE

Yes, everything changed about 1.8 million years ago when most *Homotherium* cats went extinct in Africa, and the survivors moved into the Middle East. We're not sure what happened, but one theory is that while some *Homo erectus* stayed behind in Africa, others followed the cats and other migrating animals on a big adventure, and wandered into a new continent. Eventually their descendants ended up halfway around the world!

HALFWAY AROUND THE WORLD, BRENNA?! How on earth am I meant to fit a million years of migration and half the planet's geography into this short chapter?!

OHHHH, I FORGOT I HAD A FAST-FORWARD BUTTON! Hold on tight – this is gonna be bumpy…

FAST-FORWARD BUTTON

Soooooo ... 1.8 million years ago *Homo erectus* migrate north out of Africa, travelling through the Middle East, until their descendants are 2,500 miles away in Georgia (between Türkiye and Russia). They split up and go in opposite directions, following wandering herds of animals. One bunch heads south-east and a few hundred thousand years later, their descendants reach Indonesia (a whopping 5,000 miles away from Georgia). Do they stop here? OF COURSE NOT! They split up again, and some of them head north to China. However, remember the *erectus* who headed the other way out of Georgia? Well, they're heading west for Spain, which is pretty much as far away from China as you can get without walking straight into the sea! By 800,000 years ago, *erectus* are hanging out in many parts of Europe, Africa, the Middle East and Asia. Sure, it's taken them a million years, but this amazing ability to keep adapting to changing climates, new foods, new dangers and new locations is mightily impressive! In fact, their brains are gradually getting bigger too, which might explain why they're so good at this... THE END!

Phew, what a trip! And *Homo erectus* have seen some spectacular sights on their travels. In Georgia they meet a tasty new species of huge cattle called bison, and a huge elephant called a mammoth! Although they're delicious, these plant-eaters charge around in big herds and can easily trample *erectus*, so the safest thing is to let big cats hunt them instead and scavenge the leftovers. In Europe they also find harmless deer and not-at-all harmless cave bears!

All in all, they've stumbled across a delightful selection of mostly edible animals. Which is good, because we've arrived at 780,000 years ago, and something extremely important is about to happen. Are you ready? Are you steady? Are you … *hungry*?

Yes, it's time for the first ever barbecue! Pass the ketchup, please…

5

A NICE COOKED MEAL

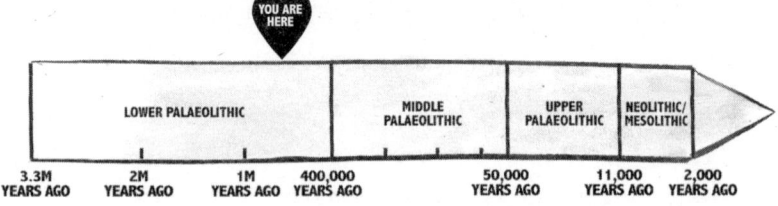

You've probably eaten cooked food your whole life, right? Me too. But here in the early Stone Age, everything is eaten raw! Sure, dinner might be served warm, but only because it's fresh meat ripped from an animal's hot-blooded body. Hominins can't cook because they don't know how. But one day, they make an exciting discovery!

Gross!

While banging flints together to make a tool, sparks shoot out and accidentally ignite the dry grass – and hey, presto, FIRE! This will change everything when it comes to food preparation. Obviously, there are no restaurants here in the Stone Age, but – if we use a hefty dose of imagination – a visit might have gone something like this…

We don't know this for sure! They may have also used wildfire from lightning strikes.

36

FLAME-GRILLED FEASTING AT THE STONE AGE STEAKHOUSE

Home to the freshest cooking techniques!

We serve all your favourite meats in a totally new way – by *cooking them*. It's where we use recently discovered *fire* to make your meat easier to chew and quicker to digest! Fire is very exciting to watch, and the food tastes absolutely delicious. Unfortunately, we have had some … uh … minor "accidents",* so please read this safety briefing before your meal.

Do not touch the fire!

The flames flicker in a hypnotic way, and you will want to reach out to touch them – DON'T! Also, it turns out that hair burns really easily, so please don't try to wear the fire as a funny hat.

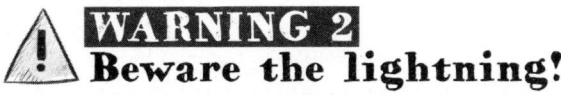
Beware the lightning!

Sometimes fire just randomly shows up thanks to scary bolts of lightning making the trees go all flamey. DO NOT TRY TO HUG THE LIGHTNING: YOU WILL DIE!

*Several people died horribly.

WARNING 3
Watch out for the hyenas!

Due to an unfortunate booking error, you're seated at the same table as a pack of ferocious hyenas. They're hungry, they've got huge teeth, and they don't want to get the sharing platter with you … so you're going to have to fight them off if you want to enjoy the mammoth meat! Good luck with that…

WARNING 4
Avoid liver poisoning!

If you kill those hyenas, DO NOT EAT THEIR LIVERS! Eating the livers of meat-eating animals seems to make hominins die horribly. However, if the animal mostly eats grass – such as a mammoth – its liver is absolutely fine.

WARNING 5
Bears beware!

If you order the fish course, watch out for bears in the river. They may look adorable, but they will rip your guts out! And it should be obvious, but if you want to sit at the edge of rivers and lakes to catch seafood, try not to fall in. We are tired of rescuing customers from the water!

WARNING 6
Having friends for dinner

You're welcome to invite friends for dinner, but be warned: they might want to have YOU for dinner! Yes, here in the Stone Age, some hominins have been known to eat other hominins. Due to recent customer complaints, we are introducing a "no nibbling" rule. Eat the mammoth meat, not your fellow diners!

On the menu ...
EVERYTHING!

Offal, brains, guts, eyeballs, bone marrow, meat – nothing goes to waste!

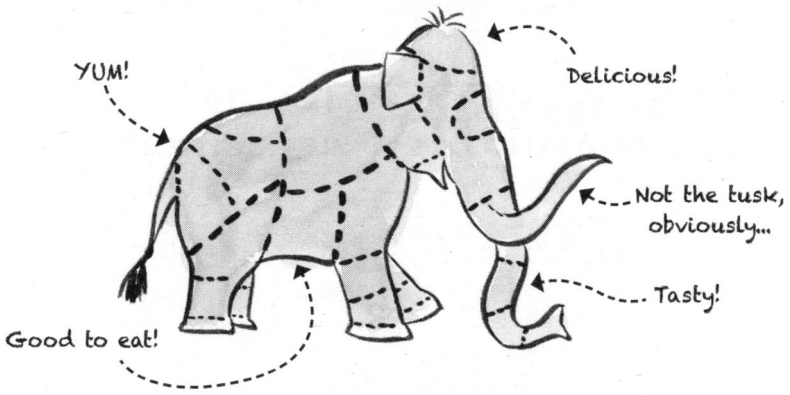

Our chefs are the finest scimitar-toothed cats in the land, and they catch the freshest animals for you to enjoy. But cats aren't great with cutlery, so you will need to break the bones and slice the meat yourself with the double-sided hand axes provided.

As long as you avoid the cats, the hyenas, the bears, the lightning, the drowning, the flames and the poisonous livers, everything should be totally delicious.

Bon appétit!

Hominin bones have been found showing human teeth marks and marks from stone tools. They must have been eaten by their friends – or enemies!

Hmm, on second thoughts I'm not sure this is my kind of restaurant! I don't love the idea of having to wrestle hyenas and vultures for my meal, and I'm even less keen on being eaten by a fellow hominin! And don't get me started on the actual menu … I mean, offal, brains, bone marrow, eyeballs? It sounds GROSS!

ACCURACY ALARM

BEEEEEEEP! BEEEEEEEP!

TELLING THE TOOTH

It might sound gross to you, Greg, but discovering how to cook meat was HUGELY important for human evolution. And one of the clearest ways we can see this is in our teeth! Some animals (called herbivores) eat only plants, and some (called carnivores) eat only meat. But early hominins, like *Homo erectus*, were omnivores ("everything-eaters"!), thanks to their teeth that were much like ours. Each tooth has a different job, perfected by evolution: incisors are for nibbling; pointy canines are for stabbing and ripping; premolars are to grind up food; and molars are for serious chewing! Other animals have to chew their food a lot more than us, and it takes way more effort to digest – just ask a cow, with its chunky teeth and four-compartment stomach! Basically, cooked food and smart teeth gave hominins a serious advantage.

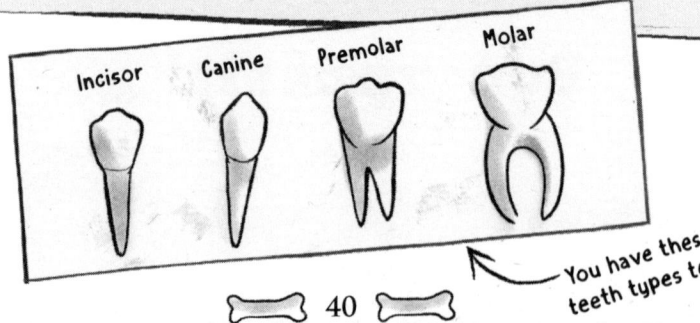

Incisor Canine Premolar Molar

You have these teeth types too!

So *Homo erectus'* new cooking skills mean less chewing and faster digestion – which means their stomachs are gradually evolving to be smaller, and all that extra energy is going to the brain instead!

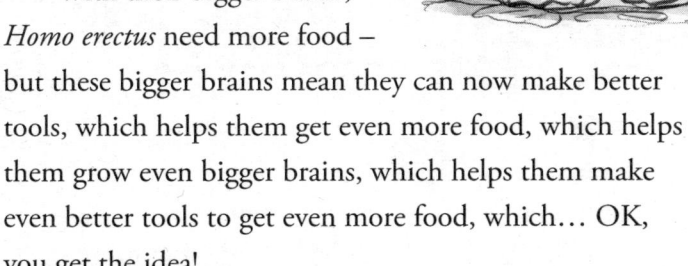

With their bigger brains, *Homo erectus* need more food – but these bigger brains mean they can now make better tools, which helps them get even more food, which helps them grow even bigger brains, which helps them make even better tools to get even more food, which… OK, you get the idea!

That's a lot to get our teeth into! It really seems like *Homo erectus* have this surviving the Stone Age thing figured out. I reckon things should stay pretty calm now, so we can just sit tight and wait for *Homo sapiens* to show up. Right?!

Er, not quite!

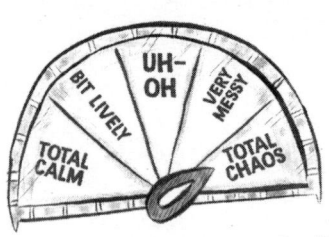

6

THE MUDDLE IN THE MIDDLE!

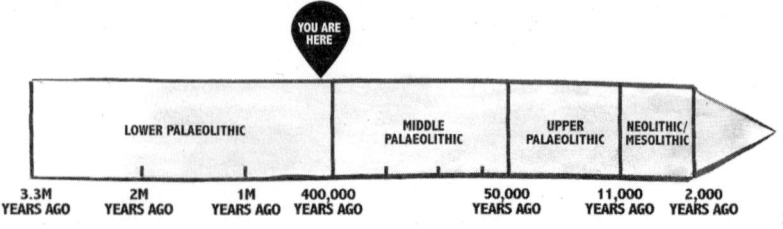

Things are going swimmingly for *Homo erectus*, who are exploring Europe powered by their new-found cooking skills. So why is my chaos meter pinging?! Wait a second – who's that over there?

OH NO!!! Don't tell me there are even MORE hominins to get to grips with?!

HEIDI HI!

Sorry, Greg, you've just crashed right into a hugely confusing bit of the Stone Age. This was a time of constant climate change, which makes the evolutionary science hard to understand — in fact, the period's proper name is the Middle Pleistocene era, but we nickname it the "muddle in the middle"! New hominin species suddenly appeared all over the place, in Africa, Europe and Asia — and they were all a little different from *Homo erectus*. One of them is often called *Homo heidelbergensis* — I like to nickname them Heidi! But we're not even sure if they were a distinct species at all. Scientists love having a big argument about this question!

Oh great, it was all going so well, but now we've been plunged into total chaos! This mysterious new species — *Homo heidelbergensis* — is coming up with their own exciting innovations. I can see a group of them building shelters that are propped up by wooden tent poles. Wow, I've not seen *erectus* do this — I think *heidelbergensis* just invented camping! I wonder if they can also invent toasted marshmallows?

They were first discovered near the German city of Heidelberg.

NO! Roughly 499,800 years too early for those, Greg!

BREAKING INTO BRITAIN

And that's not all. These happy campers also seem to be keen explorers. They have made it all the way to Britain, which is fun for me because that's where I live, and...

We've found footprints and tools in Britain from an unknown Homo species who arrived 900,000 years ago – someone got there before Heidi!

Wait, Britain is an island, so how did they cross the sea? HANG ON, WHERE IS THE SEA?! CALL THE POLICE! SOMEONE HAS STOLEN THE ENGLISH CHANNEL!!!

ACCURACY ALARM

BEEEEEEEP! BEEEEEEP!

NO SEA TO SEE!

Ah, I forgot to tell you. When *Homo heidelbergensis* first visited Britain, about 500,000 years ago, the island was connected to mainland Europe by a thin strip of land, so it wasn't an island yet! Even more surprisingly, Britain was home to lots of animals that don't live there any more, like rhinos, elephants, lions, bears, hyenas and hippos!

OK, let me try to get a handle on this chaos: *Homo heidelbergensis* are wandering round a Britain that isn't even an island, and is home to <u>hippos!</u> But don't get used to it, because everything's changing again – it's suddenly turning cold. REALLY cold!

Prehistoric hippo bones were found under London's Trafalgar Square!

A huge ice sheet is now covering Britain and sending hominins scurrying back to mainland Europe – that's right, we're in an ICE AGE! What a chaotic climate!

Don't worry if you forgot to pack your woolly hat, because this Ice Age only lasts 50,000 years, and it's warming up again now. With glorious sunshine back in Britain, hominins are returning – and they're bringing something very exciting with them. After 3 million years of scavenging for food, hominins have come up with a revolutionary new bit of tech that means they can, at long last, HUNT animals! It's—

About every 100,000 years it would get REALLY cold in some places and cause an Ice Age.

Hi! Are you bored of waiting for scimitar-toothed cats to finish their feasts?

FANCY HUNTING FOR YOUR-SELF?

Come down to Tool Shed to check out our latest invention:

THE SPEAR!

It's the future! Perfect for jabbing and stabbing animals from a safe distance. It'll change your life!

(WARNING: If the wooden spear snaps, it might end your life too. Always bring a spare spear.)

PICK ONE UP TODAY!

Gah! Stupid adverts. I can't close them fast enough—

Speared your animal? Process its meat and fur more easily with our patented knapping innovation:

THE LEVALLOIS TECHNIQUE!

With our new technique, we craft each little flint flake until it's perfect for all your nicey-slicey-dicey needs!

> The oldest spear ever found is 400,000 years old from Clacton, England. Only the 39 cm long sharpened tip survives; the shaft had snapped off.

Yeesh! Always be careful about believing what adverts promise you, because they don't tell you the downsides: it doesn't matter how sharp your spear is when a four-tonne mammoth is charging at you!

Although hunting may have its dangers, as we emerge from this time of chaos, it's a huge step forward for hominins. They can hunt massive beasts by scaring them off cliffs or catching them in traps. I don't know about you, but I'm glad I can get all my food in a safe supermarket...

WHEEEEEEEEK!

WHEEEEEEEEEEEEEEK!

Uh ... can you hear a weird shrieking sound? Is it some sort of furious bird? Wait ... that's not you, is it, Brenna? Nah, it sounds like nothing I've heard before. Hmm, I wonder what it is?

Rude! ↘

MEET THE NEANDERTHALS!

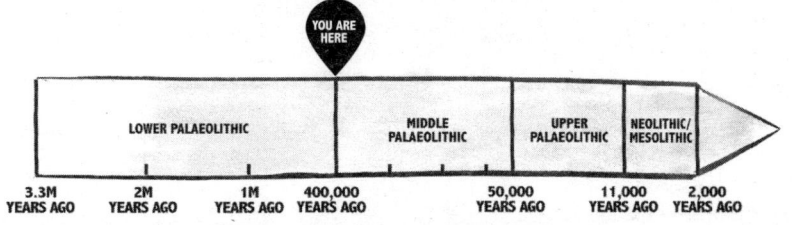

I FIGURED OUT WHAT THE WEIRD NOISE IS!!!
We've met so many *Homo* species already, but at last, 400,000 years ago, we've bumped into one that you might have heard of: Neanderthals!

Homo neanderthalensis to be scientific.

Yes, they've shown up here in Europe with some cool new ideas, some new spears, and a distinctively weird shrieking sound! I think we should go and check them out. We certainly know what to listen out for, but what are we looking for?

SPOT THE NEANDERTHAL!

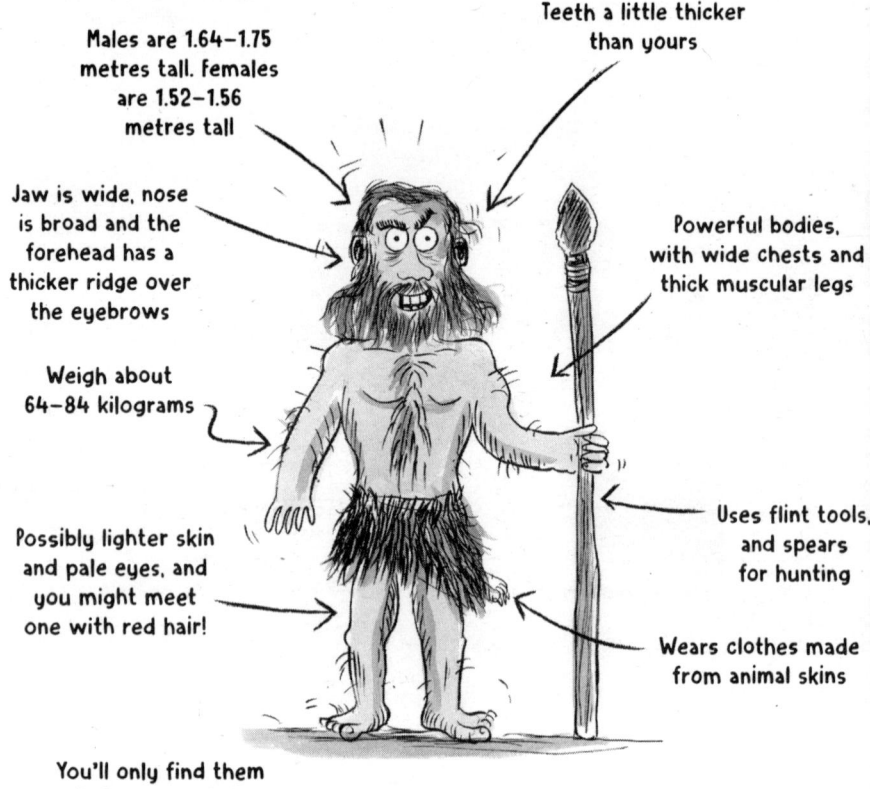

Males are 1.64–1.75 metres tall, females are 1.52–1.56 metres tall

Teeth a little thicker than yours

Jaw is wide, nose is broad and the forehead has a thicker ridge over the eyebrows

Powerful bodies, with wide chests and thick muscular legs

Weigh about 64–84 kilograms

Possibly lighter skin and pale eyes, and you might meet one with red hair!

Uses flint tools, and spears for hunting

Wears clothes made from animal skins

You'll only find them in Europe or Asia

Although you may have heard of Neanderthals before, I'm guessing it hasn't all been positive? They have a pretty dodgy reputation in modern culture, and they are famous for being stupid, violent and totally different from us *Homo sapiens*. Is this all true, or do we need to bust some myths? Brenna, over to you!

8

MYTH BUSTER: Neanderthals!

MYTH BUSTER 1

NEANDERTHALS WERE STUPID

We've never found a fossilized Neanderthal brain, but their skulls had space for slightly bigger brains than our own. They probably weren't stupid at all! But the big question is: HOW did they think? We don't know if their brains were wired to do the same jobs as ours. Maybe their bigger brains supported bigger eyes to see better in the dark winters of northern Europe or inside gloomy caves? We also don't know if Neanderthals were good at social relationships. We *Homo sapiens* are very good at this, thanks to a part of our brain called the frontal cortex. But Neanderthal skulls had less room in that area – did that affect their social skills?

We do know Neanderthals made very cool tools from bone, antler and wood. They required a lot of skill to craft, meaning Neanderthals were smart and patient. Neanderthals also possibly figured out how to make glue from tree bark, which requires a super-complicated process of burning the wood at just the right temperature – they must have been masters of managing a campfire!

MYTH BUSTER 2

NEANDERTHALS WERE VIOLENT BRUTES

They were certainly built like rugby-playing bruisers, but those stocky bodies, strong arms and thick thighs likely evolved to deal with climate change instead of punch-ups! In fact, Neanderthals could be very caring. We know that at least one Neanderthal – or maybe even a whole family – looked after a man we now call Shanidar 1. He had many injuries – he'd lost an eye and some of his hearing, and his right arm was withered. Yet he survived into middle age because he had support. However, we also found another body, called Shanidar 3, with a hole in his rib that might have been from a stabbing! So maybe Neanderthals were just like modern humans: a strange mixture of really kind and brutally horrible, depending on the day!

That's my BFF!

NEANDERTHALS WERE CAVEMEN

Well, obviously half of them weren't men, otherwise they wouldn't have survived very long as a species! Did they only live in caves? Nope! Neanderthals lived all over the place, often out in open plains where animals were grazing and water was easily found. Caves and rock overhangs would have been great places to shelter, but the reason we think about Neanderthals as cavemen – or rather, cave people! – is because their bones and tools survived better in caves for us to find, whereas out in the open they got buried or were disturbed by wild animals.

NEANDERTHALS ONLY LIVED IN THE ICE AGE

We used to think this was true! Scientists argued their bodies were especially well adapted for living in cold places. But most modern experts will tell you the evidence shows they preferred a warmer climate.

Also, it wasn't THE Ice Age. As we've already seen in Britain, during the Stone Age the weather kept changing, so there were LOTS of Ice Ages – and WARM ages too! Average temperatures were often 2-4 degrees hotter than today, but sudden cold snaps would cover everything in ice. Within one person's lifetime, glaciers could freeze and melt again. Sadly there's no movie called *Warm Age* starring Scrat the nut-obsessed, sabre-toothed squirrel rat!

MYTH BUSTER 5: NEANDERTHALS DIDN'T KNOW HOW TO MAKE CLOTHES

This is partially a myth – Neanderthals knew how to scrape animal skins to make fur coverings for warmth. But they didn't know how to sew with a needle, which is what allowed for closer-fitting clothes that came later.

Neanderthals may have tanned leather hides to get certain colours. They possibly also burnished the skins, like we do with leather to waterproof it. Very recently, archaeologists found little balls of yarn from 50,000 years ago, made from the fibres of tree bark. This may have allowed Neanderthals to attach tools to their belts, or bags to carry stuff in. Finally, there's decent evidence of Neanderthals making jewellery from shells and bird talons, so maybe they liked to accessorize their outfits!

MYTH BUSTER 6
NEANDERTHALS DIDN'T HAVE ART

We used to say this a lot, but now it's debatable. We know Neanderthals were able to get beautiful colour pigments from powdered rocks. They had a choice of red, brown, black and yellow, and they rubbed rocks so that colourful streaks were left behind, a bit like crayons you'd give to a toddler! It's possible they also made their own paints by mixing bones with traces of minerals. Were these colours a bit of fun? Were they practical? Was this Neanderthal suncream? Medicine? Or camouflage to help them hide when hunting animals? We don't know!

But there are some interesting discoveries in caves that could be Neanderthal art. Circles made 175,000 years ago from hundreds of little bits of broken stalactites and stalagmites (stalactites are like stony icicles hanging down from cave ceilings; stalagmites stick up from cave floors) have been found in Bruniquel Cave in France! No animal could have done this, so why did Neanderthals bother?

It suggests they enjoyed making interesting patterns. Plus, a bold new theory argues Neanderthals stencilled their hands on the walls of Spanish caves 66,000 years ago. Lots of experts aren't convinced, though, because dating paints or minerals from so long ago is very hard.

MYTH BUSTER 7

WE ARE DESCENDED FROM NEANDERTHALS

We're not direct descendants – we're more like cousins! However, there was a hugely exciting shock when scientists analysed Neanderthal DNA (DNA is the secret code in cells for building any animal – I'll tell you more about it later in the book!). They realized that *Homo sapiens* and Neanderthals had previously had children together! In fact, many modern people – including you and me, Greg – have between 1 and 4% Neanderthal DNA! People with African heritage probably won't have any because Neanderthals only lived in Europe and Asia. So there is a surprising human/Neanderthal connection!

MYTHS BUSTED!

Wow, thanks very much, Brenna! It seems Neanderthals are way smarter and more interesting than many people assume. And – best of all – if Neanderthals are finally here, then surely modern humans must be on the way soon! At last we can stop messing around with all these other types of hominin and just focus on the story of our own species, good ol' *Homo sapiens*...

And I can hear a commotion coming from Russia – surely this is our ancestors getting up and running? Hooray!

ACCURACY ALARM

BEEEEEEEP! BEEEEEEEP!

NEW SPECIES ALERT!

Sorry, Greg – *Homo sapiens* are still not here yet! This is a totally different species – yes, another one! We've only just discovered them and they're a bit of a mystery, so maybe you should start a new chapter...

Urgh, typical! OK, here we go again...

9
SPECIES SURPRISE!

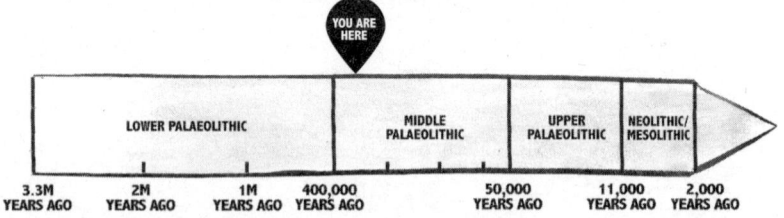

Well, I guess I should get used to being wrong, because every time I think we're done with new species, another one pops up out of nowhere! We've now got to head over to a cave in Siberia, in Russia, to meet yet another new arrival: *Homo denisova*, or Denisovans!

Now, I'd love to tell you all about this new species of hominin roaming around West and East Asia but, er … well, they're a bit mysterious. I guess the only thing we can say for certain is they're all called Dennis or Denise?

ACCURACY ALARM

HOMO DENISOVA IS DENIS-OVER THERE!

No, Greg! Denisovans are named after the cave in Siberia where they were found. This species is mysterious because all we have discovered is a handful of small bones and teeth. These bones barely tell us anything about how tall they were, or how they walked, or what they looked like. In fact, for a while, our only evidence they existed was a 50,000-year-old teeny-tiny bone from a young girl's fingertip. Nobody expected it to be special — finger bones all look alike! However, in 2010, scientists ran it through a brilliant new technology called DNA sequencing and they got a surprise! Her DNA revealed she was from a brand-new species. Normally, DNA doesn't survive from the deep Stone Age, because hot and wet conditions damage it, but *Homo denisova* was found in a cold, dry cave, so they got amazingly lucky.

Wow, science is awesome! OK, so Denisovans are sharing the planet with Neanderthals, *heidelbergensis*, and *erectus*. SURELY it'll be *Homo sapiens* coming along next, yeah?

Wait, hang on… Who's that?!

NOT ANOTHER ONE

Homo naledi was only found in 2013 because brave cavers dislocated their own shoulders to squeeze through a tiny gap! Don't do this at home, kids!

Bear with me, because there's ANOTHER new species to tell you about: *Homo naledi*. But the funny thing is, they don't look new. In fact, *Homo naledi* is … TINY! They've got a little skull, a much dinkier brain and waddle-walking hips like an ape – and they're so much shorter and skinnier than Neanderthals!

BLAST FROM THE PAST

You might assume that evolution progresses forward in a logical way, but remember that it's actually totally chaotic! Even though *erectus*, *heidelbergensis*, Neanderthals and Denisovans have increasingly looked more like us, sometimes evolution seems to go sideways or even backwards. *Homo naledi* dates to only 335,000 years ago, but looks like a much earlier Australopithecine species from 4 million years ago!

WOW! I really didn't see that coming. I was so sure we'd meet *Homo sapiens* next, and yet the evolutionary engine now seems to be in reverse gear! Honestly, at this rate, are modern humans EVER going to show up?! I'm starting to give up hope, and—

WAIT ... I'm sure I just saw a familiar face pop out of a cave. Hang on, let me get a closer look. I've been wrong before, and I don't want to look like a fool again…

Hmm, you know what? I'm satisfied! I think it's FINALLY HAPPENED! It's taken millions of years, and loads of really bizarre detours, but at last I think we can say hello to …

Homo sapiens **has entered the chat**

10
HELLO, HOMO SAPIENS

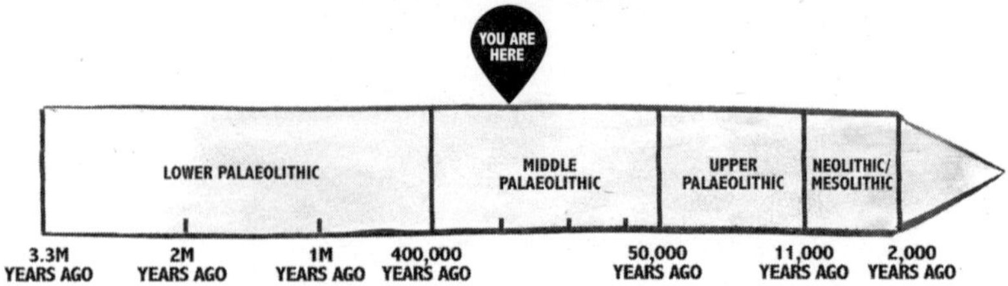

It may have taken us millions of years, but *Homo sapiens* – or as we call them, humans – have finally evolved on planet Earth. Huzzah!

And I don't need to tell you what they look like, because they look just like you! They're modern humans with our high domed and rounded skulls, flatter faces, narrower noses and – most important of all – a brand-new feature never seen before in other *Homo* species...

THE MIGHTY HUMAN CHIN!

It's true; only Homo sapiens seem to have evolved this chin shape!

Homo sapiens are super smart, super handy, super adaptable and super keen on learning new things. In fact, they're just like you and me in every biological way. Oh, except for one crucial thing: at this early stage, humans haven't yet learned how to talk...

ACCURACY ALARM

I disagree, Greg! I think even this long ago, humans could talk. In fact, I reckon Neanderthals and Denisovans could talk too...

Ohhh, really?! Sounds like we have a huge difference of opinion, because I've read lots of books saying Neanderthals definitely couldn't talk. Hmm, there's only one way to handle this – with a big argument!!! Fire up the moody music and bright studio lights, it's time for...

Let's go!

HISTORIAN HEAD-TO-HEAD

Two experts, two different theories: who will be the winner? Let's get ready to rumble!

ROUND 1
WHAT IS "TALKING", ANYWAY?

Monkeys and apes communicate with sounds and grunts, and the famous gorilla named Koko even learned sign language. If you take an ape brain and add in 7 million years of evolution, I think it's likely that Neanderthals, Denisovans and *sapiens* could all make mouth sounds to share ideas and instructions with others. That's talking!

Yeah, maybe they had words for useful things - *cave, fire, mammoth*, etc. Perhaps they even vocalized certain patterns, like chirping songbirds. But complex language skills are way harder! That's when each word has its own special meaning (called semantics) and also when you change word order to create new meanings (called syntax). If I say "the dog ate my homework", I'm making excuses to my teacher; but if I say "the homework ate my dog", I'm in a horror movie! Animals can communicate but they can't do wordplay!

Actually, modern research suggests birds probably CAN do semantics and syntax! Maybe not as brilliantly as us, but it's an old-fashioned idea that only humans can talk. The more we study animals, the more we realize how smart they are. So I think early humans were capable of being pretty chatty!

ROUND 2
WHAT CAN WE LEARN FROM PREHISTORIC SKELETONS?

If you're telling me you think Neanderthals could talk, we need to look at how our bodies produce sounds – and I don't mean embarrassing noises from our bums!

Gross, Greg! Humans can speak thanks to an organ in our throat called the larynx, which has our vocal cords inside. Different sounds are also made by moving the tongue. There's also the hyoid bone above the larynx that's important for swallowing and speech. For a long while, experts thought Neanderthals had the hyoid bone in a different position to us, but recently we discovered that's not true – which means they could probably speak like us!

I didn't know that! OK, fair enough, but let's talk tongues. Unlike chimps, human tongues are round (not flat), sit at the back of our mouths and continue down our throats. This gives us a bigger range of sounds. We can make various mouth clicks (they're used in some African languages), but also trickier sounds like "cuhhhh", "eeeeeeh" and "ooooh". Chimps don't make these noises. Neanderthal skeletons show their tongues were further forward than ours, so maybe they also struggled with these complex sounds?

Actually, new research tells us chimps CAN make those sounds – they just don't want to! So, maybe it didn't matter where the Neanderthal tongue was? Plus, their ears were shaped a lot like ours, so they might have heard the same sorts of sounds as us – cheerful chitchat, and people complaining about the weather!

But there is an important difference between us and Neanderthals: they had bigger, barrel-shaped chests. All that extra space meant they were probably much louder than humans. One theory is they hummed rather than spoke; another theory says their voices sounded like loud, high-pitched shrieks! So, even if they did talk (which I don't think they did!), it would have been SO ANNOYING! Imagine gossiping with a Neanderthal at the back of the classroom – everyone would hear all your secrets!

ROUND 3
WHAT ABOUT BRAINS?

I'll admit we don't know if Neanderthals had the same brain layout as us, with the areas for processing language. Their brains were generally larger than ours, though!

Yes, but human skulls give more space to the prefrontal cortex at the front of the brain. This does loads of jobs, but it also helps out with speech. Neanderthals had lower foreheads, so maybe their front brain was less developed?

Disagree! Evidence suggests the prefrontal cortex had already developed in earlier species of *Homo* (but not in chimps).

Yeah, BUT early *Homo sapiens* still used the same old tools as other hominins. Humans are amazing inventors, so why hadn't they invented anything better by this point? I reckon it's because they didn't yet have language - therefore, neither did Neanderthals! I think speech emerged later, when climate change forced humans to work together to survive. After that the cool stuff was invented, like art and music.

What if they had art and music earlier, and we just haven't found proof yet? We're constantly finding new evidence! Based on what we know so far, I think early *Homo sapiens* AND Neanderthals were chatterboxes.

Thanks Brenna, that was fun – even if we don't have all the answers! Don't worry, reader, it's normal for historians, archaeologists and scientists to disagree over the same evidence. One day we might find new techniques or new evidence to answer these mysteries.

Whether they're chatting or not, *Homo sapiens* are finally here, and they're starting to develop new and improved tools—

NEW FROM TOOL SHED!

WITH STATE-OF-THE-ART HAFTING TECHNOLOGY

Introducing the revolutionary
FLINT-TIPPED SPEAR

Getting annoyed when your spear blunts on thick hippo hide?

Worry no more with our exciting attachable gadget! Our stronger, sharper flint blade gives even greater poking power!

We think this invention arrived 200,000 years ago, possibly earlier.

GAAAAHHHH! Stupid adverts ruining my book!

But, in fairness, <u>hafting</u> does sound pretty sensible. It's a way of attaching a flint blade to a wooden handle that makes hunting weapons sharper and stronger. It's a great innovation by *Homo sapiens* and maybe it's even something that other *Homo* species are able to learn.

Anyway, whether or not Neanderthals and humans can talk, at this point in our story they certainly can't chat to each other – they've not met yet! Humans live in Africa, and Neanderthals only live in Europe and West Asia. But remember there are still other species of *Homo* bouncing around the planet.

In fact, guess what? A new one just turned up … again! Prepare yourself for a big *little* surprise!

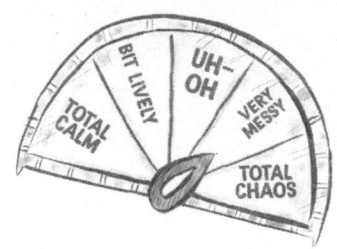

11

HOW MANY HOMININS?!

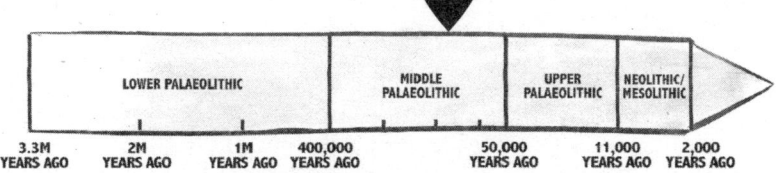

Now that *Homo sapiens* have finally shown up, the planet is bursting with different species of hominins. Don't worry, I'm finding it hard to keep track too! Before we recap, we have ONE more to meet. Let's head over to a massive collection of islands in South East Asia. These islands are very remote, and surrounded by dangerous waves. It's amazing hominins have managed to get here at all! Maybe they were carried here in the beaks of giant seagulls, or rode here on the back of sharks. Or, you know, maybe they did something boring like building a raft...

Together they're known as the country of Indonesia.

This is a big debate! It's definitely not the sharks or seagulls, though...

Now we've finally waded ashore on the island of Flores, we find ourselves face to face with the new species: *Homo floresiensis*. Or maybe not quite face to face, as the fascinating thing about this species is they are very small! They're just over a metre tall when fully grown.

And look over there – there's a mini elephant, too! What's going on here? Have we stumbled across some kind of hobbit island?

We found *Homo floresiensis'* tools from 190,000 years ago, but we've only found their bones from 100,000 years ago.

Small but perfectly formed!

ACCURACY ALARM · BEEEEEEP! · BEEEEEEP ·

ALL THE SMALL THINGS

Actually, scientists did nickname *Homo floresiensis* "hobbits" (after the little heroes in J.R.R. Tolkien's fantasy books). Experts first wondered if these were *Homo sapiens* with a medical growth condition called dwarfism. However, scientists later found mini versions of other animals too, including a shrunken elephant called a *Stegodon* which was hunted by the small hominins. It's a great example of island dwarfism, where evolution shrinks species down so they can better survive in cramped places.

HOMO-SIDE-BY-SIDE

Right, now we've met *Homo floresiensis,* let's try to get our heads round all these hominins sharing the planet. In fact, it would be easier to look at them all together, like in a police line-up of suspects. Instead of a homicide investigation, it's a *Homo*-side-by-side investigation!

Homicide is what police call a murder.

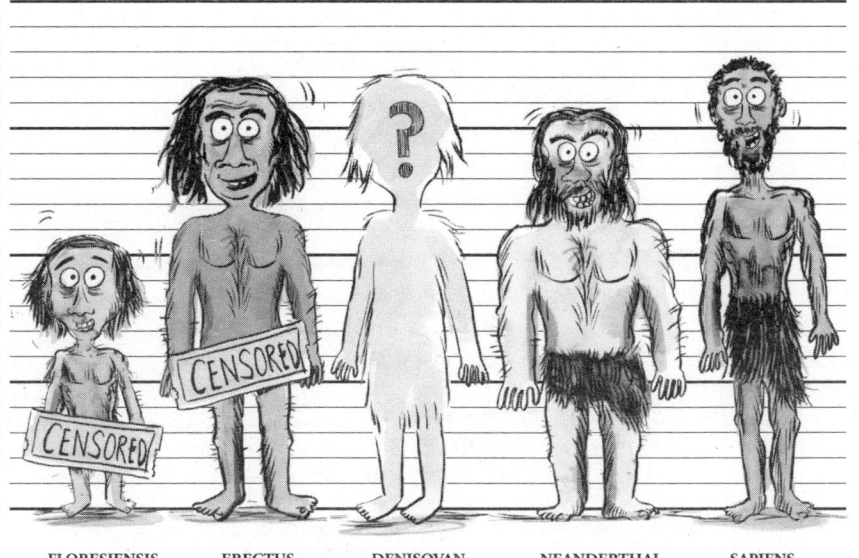

190,000 years ago

FLORESIENSIS	ERECTUS	DENISOVAN	NEANDERTHAL	SAPIENS
1.10 m	1.70 m	1.70 m	1.60 m	1.75 m
SOUTH EAST ASIA	SOUTH EAST ASIA	WEST & EAST ASIA	EUROPE & WEST ASIA	EAST AFRICA

Wait! Aren't there meant to be seven species in that line-up?

Oh drat! Looks like *Homo heidelbergensis* and *Homo naledi* have both gone extinct! This leaves us with a neat collection of five kinds of hominins.

FIVE-ISH

Sorry, Greg, it's not that neat! There might actually be six. You see, in 1933 an ancient skull was found in China, near the Longjiang (Dragon) River. Because of war and politics, the skull remained a secret until 2018. Scientists then realized it was 150,000 years old, and called it *Homo longi* (but nicknamed it "Dragon Man" – SO COOL!). However, some scientists think Dragon Man is actually just *Homo denisova*. Unfortunately, we can't prove it because DNA testing has failed so far. So I don't actually know if *longi* is a new species or not!

How mysterious! OK, so there's five (maybe six!) species of hominins – but we're nearly halfway through the book and there's still way too much to cram in. Sorry, but I'm going to have to jump forward over 100,000 years: WHOOOOOOOOOSH!

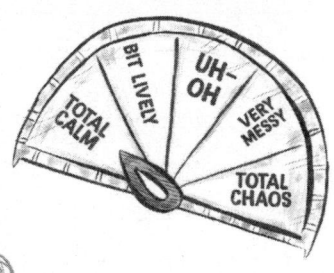

12
LOOKING COOL IN THE ICE AGE!

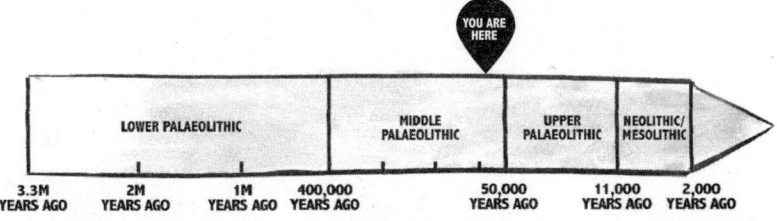

Phew, that was a lot of whooshing!!! We've raced along at breakneck speed to 80,000 years ago, and I can bring you two bits of very, very important news. First, the bad news: *Homo erectus* has gone extinct! Farewell to the most successful *Homo* species of all time; it's always sad to see a champion retire, but what a fabulous career!

← They survived until 110,000 years ago. In happier news, they didn't all "die out"; some evolved into other *Homo* species.

But please don't feel too downhearted, because I also have EXCITING NEWS: *Homo sapiens* have left Africa! Again, we must blame climate change for this grand new adventure. The summers have been heating up in Africa (honestly, is the climate ever normal in this book?!), and that has produced long corridors of lush green grasslands stretching all the way up into the Middle East. Loads of migrating animals like bats, honey badgers and porcupines have cheerfully explored these new corridors, forcing <u>some hungry humans to follow behind until they accidentally ended up in a different continent!</u>

We recently found human remains from 180,000 years ago in a cave in Israel, so this wasn't the first attempt!

Hey, where's everybody going?

OK, I must confess ... I didn't *actually* see which way they went. I'm guessing they either <u>crossed the water between East Africa and Arabia, or just walked from North Africa into the Middle East.</u>

They might have crossed a short stretch of water between East Africa and Yemen called Bab-el-Mandeb.

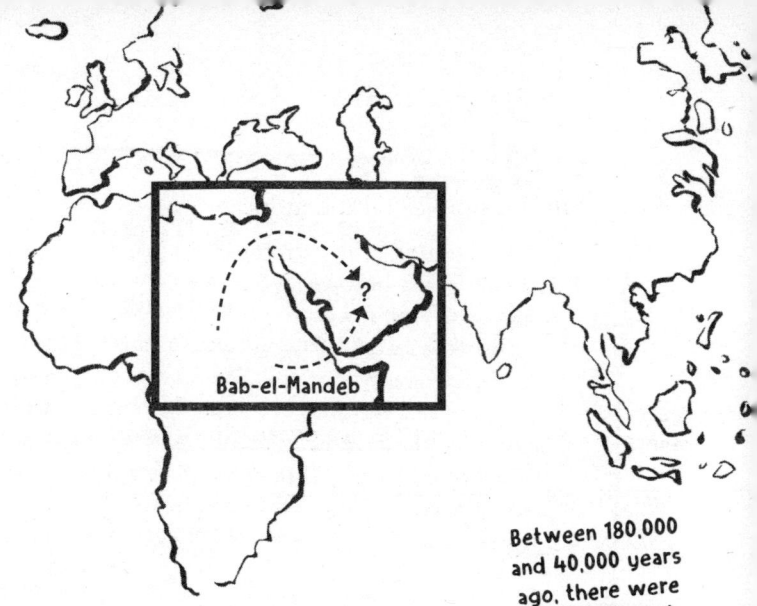

Between 180,000 and 40,000 years ago, there were many different phases of humans leaving Africa (and even some going back the other way)!

However they did it, if *Homo sapiens* are starting to explore, that means they might soon bump into Neanderthals and Denisovans. Will they play nice, or will we see hominins fighting to the death for control of hunting grounds? Stay tuned...

CHILL OUT

Now we've caught up on the latest news, let's keep moving forward. As humans head further north, it's suddenly getting very, very chilly! In fact, it looks like we're heading into another Ice Age. You might remember that we've already had an Ice Age that emptied out Britain. Well, now these Ice Ages seem to be happening even more often, and it's time for another one!

ICE ICE MAYBE

That's right – and amazingly, you can blame them on outer space! Saturn and Jupiter's gravity pulls Earth away from the Sun, stretching its orbit from circular to lemon-shaped. This affects how much solar radiation reaches us, causing an Ice Age to happen every 100,000 years! The fancy name for this pattern is Milankovitch cycles, named after the astronomer who discovered them. Crucially, Ice Ages didn't affect the whole planet – when Europe had freezing winters, Africa and Australia had mild weather all year. Fascinating, huh?

Oh, so this Ice Age isn't happening everywhere?! In that case, let's hop over to sunny South Africa, where there's no ice to worry about, and they've just invented the seafood buffet – nice! Catching shellfish is a great way to get protein, vitamins and calories. Also, it's very relaxing – they can just sit there with a harpoon and net, waiting for lunch to swim to them, instead of spending days chasing animals in the blazing hot sunshine!

80,000 years ago seems to have been when humans made a big leap forward with new ideas, new technology, and a growing population. Maybe the shellfish diet allowed more time for thinking and socializing!

So, with the weather being wildly dramatic, that presents some serious clothing challenges. Do you dress for the beach or dress for skiing? Handily enough, humans have just got really into their fashion – let's get some tips!

GET THE
LOOK

Beady? Aye!
The latest thing: shell jewellery!

The bear necessities
Fur: the only must-have trend this year!

Sew amazing!
The brand-new *Homo sapien* invention!

Wanna look cool while staying warm? Need the fiercest looks for your summer cave aesthetic? Don't stress! If you wanna slay while you vacay, or look niiiiiice in the ice, we're your year-round fashion bible, bringing you the hottest trends from the coolest locations!

COULD YOU BEAD ANY TRENDIER?

Hanging out in the warm caves of southern Africa? Then get yourself the latest thing: shell jewellery! Simply hang shells from your clothes, belt or body – it's up to you how you style them. You can even punch holes in the shells with a sharp tool and then thread them with twisted plant fibres. So cute! They're so beautiful, so small and so fiddly to make… Omigod we are OBSESSSED!

Want more accessory inspiration? Try a burst of colour. You can make your own paint by grinding up the pigments in the giant shells you find at the beach. All you need is a liquid to mix the dusty rock into a sticky paste. May we suggest wee? Home-made ingredients are perfect for that all-natural aesthetic, and ur-ine luck – you'll never run out of your own!

Need a paintbrush? Use a wolf's leg bone! Why not scribble patterns on your clothes, or smear it onto your own skin as sunblock, make-up or insect repellent.*

* OK, sure, we can't prove any of this actually works, but who cares when you look absolutely stunning!

THE BEAR NECESSITIES

Hey, not everyone can bask at the beach. If you left Africa for that glam glacier life, and you're struggling to look chic while you shiver, there's only one trend this year (and every year!) and that's BEAR FUR! It's the heaviest insulation you can get. Sure, the colour options are limited – it comes in brown, brown or slightly darker brown – but it's a guaranteed way to keep the frost out.

Not sure how to get a fur coat? We recommend bringing several heavily armed friends to slaughter your nearest bear; don't try it alone or you'll end up as a literal fashion victim. Once the bear is dead, slice off its skin, scrub it clean, wash it in your juiciest vat of fatty animal brains (this breaks down the skin fibres), then stretch it out, dry it over a smoky fire and buff it smooth with a rough-edged rock. It's now soft enough to wear against your skin, waterproof and super toasty!

WHO WORE IT BEST?

Introducing the brand-new *Homo sapiens* invention: sewing! It means *sapiens* can now be snug and snazzy in their tightly fitting clothes, unlike Neanderthals in their baggy animal skins. There's no *need*le to thank us – you're welcome!

THE LATEST FASHION

Humans maybe started wearing animal skins 170,000 years ago. How do we know? Because this was when head lice evolved into a new species of body lice who liked to live in clothing! The earliest evidence for sewing needles isn't until around 45,000 years ago, but there were likely simpler earlier designs made of bone or wood called awls, which did similar jobs. And it's true that even this long ago, we have evidence for *sapiens* being arty: sea snail shells filled with colourful pigments have been found at Blombos Cave in South Africa – the oldest ever evidence of art materials! In the same cave, there are rocks decorated with colourful criss-cross lines which are arguably the earliest drawings ever!

Wow! So all this fashion and art proves humans are now working smarter, not harder. They can plan multistage projects, produce different materials and think beyond simple survival.

Now that everyone looks sharp in their latest fits, it's time to show off these hot new looks ... by going on tour!

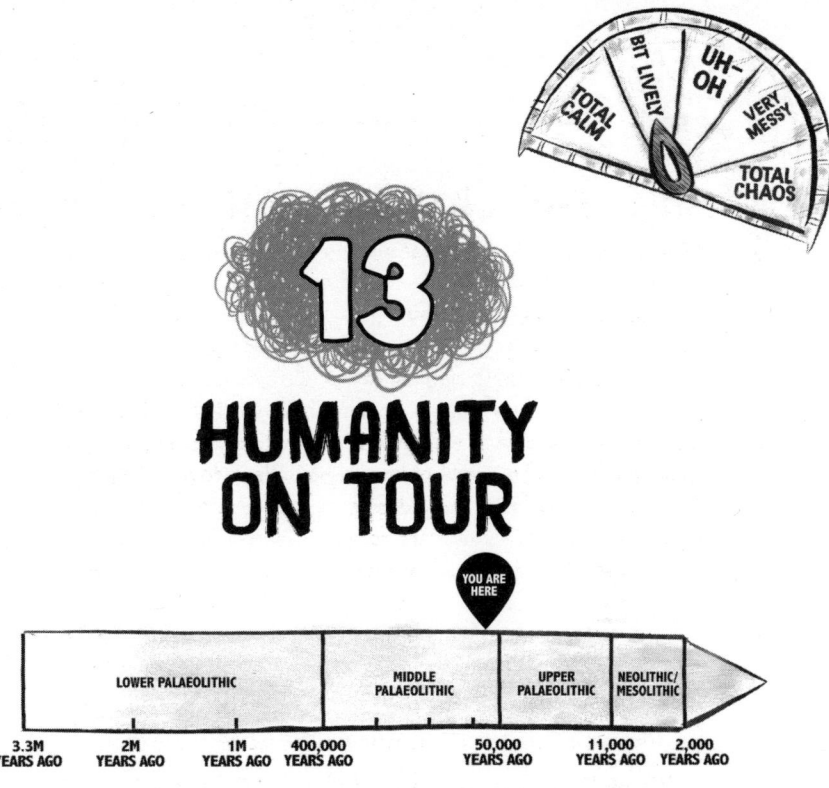

13
HUMANITY ON TOUR

Since leaving Africa and arriving in the Middle East, humans have been splitting off in different directions (just like *Homo erectus* did, all those years before). This means they're encountering new animals to hunt, new plants to eat, new landscapes to conquer, new weather patterns to understand, new challenges to tackle and … OH, NEW NEIGHBOURS TO MEET!

Hmm, let's have a quick look at the *Homo sapiens* travel itinerary, shall we?

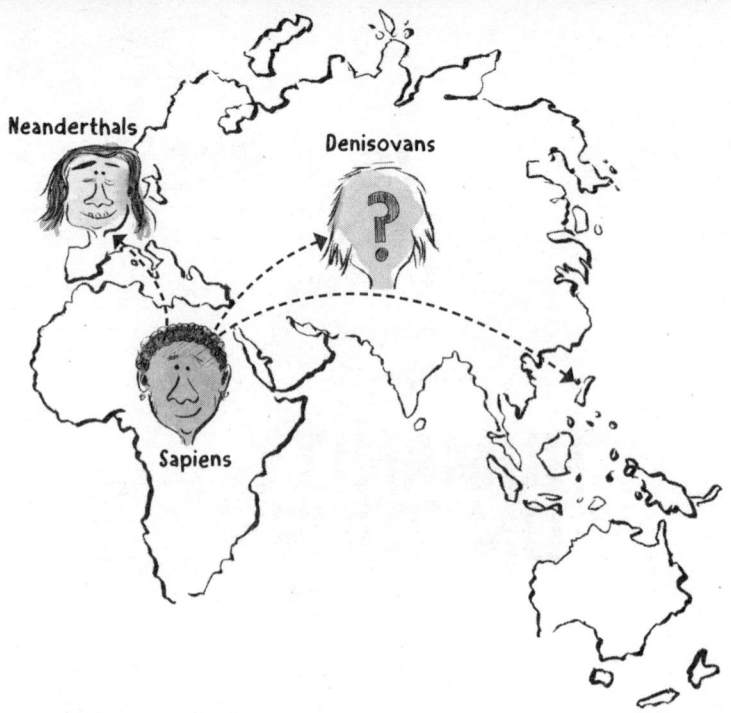

Ah, well, this is interesting! Some humans head north into the big open plains of East Asia, where they bump straight into the Denisovans – uh-oh! Will they battle to the death over control of these lands?

Amazingly, it's the opposite. Denisovans and humans start <u>having kids together!</u>

While one bunch of humans explore the Denisovan dating scene, a second batch wander westwards towards Europe, heading towards where the big, buff, brainy (and screechy) Neanderthals live. Will this be a recipe for violence, or more lovely romance?! Which species will survive? Place your bets now!

> This is called interbreeding. Having a bit of Denisovan DNA might explain why modern humans in Tibet can live high up in mountains.

EXPLOSIVE TIMES

But I want to follow the THIRD gang of *Homo sapiens*, who have walked down into South East Asia. Here they pass by a very, very, *very* big mountain which looks a bit … uh … smoky? Are mountains meant to do that?

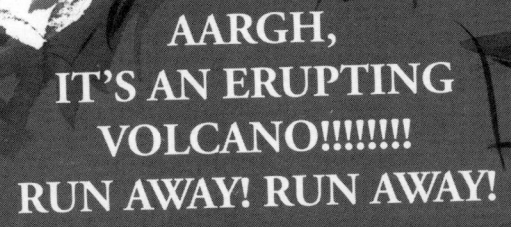

AARGH, IT'S AN ERUPTING VOLCANO!!!!!!!! RUN AWAY! RUN AWAY!

Oh no! The volcano is pumping out dirty black ash – everything has gone dark! And I bet all that sky smog will block out the sunshine and ruin the weather again, won't it? Honestly, we've already got one Ice Age under way; surely we can't face yet more chaotic climate catastrophes?

ACCURACY ALARM

BEEEEEEEP! BEEEEEEP!

VOLCANIC PANIC!

This volcano was Mount Toba on the Indonesian island of Sumatra, which erupted 74,000 years ago. It was a huge explosion, and scientists used to think its ash cloud blocked out the sun, caused environmental catastrophe and pretty much killed every human outside of Africa. But we now know they found a way to survive!

Yes, somehow humans find a way to cling on after the volcano disaster. Not only do they thrive in India and South East Asia, but if we jump to 67,000 years ago, people have now figured out how to build super-fast JET SKIS! OK, maaaaaaaaybe that's a *slight* exaggeration. But even if it's not on jet skis, humans have still managed to cross big stretches of water and paddled between the many islands of Indonesia.

NO, GREG!!! →

There's a VERY big scientific debate about how they did this. Was it boats? Log canoes? Rafts? Who knows?

I wish I had a jet ski!

Now let's head over to the Philippines, because there's ANOTHER new species of hominin here!

HOMO LUZONENSIS — NEW SPECIES

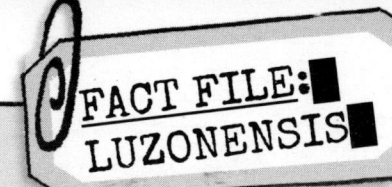

FACT FILE: LUZONENSIS

Homo luzonensis are much smaller than Homo sapiens but slightly bigger than Homo floresiensis, the "hobbits" on Flores Island. Luzonensis have a strange mix of ancient and modern features: they have small teeth like us, but the bones in their feet are closer to Australopithecus (who lived 3 million years earlier!).

WOW! Isn't it bizarre how evolution keeps chaotically churning out different types of hominins, big and small?

GOING DOWN UNDER

Right, well, that was surprising, but we're supposed to be on a world tour! Where is humanity heading next? Well, the wandering *Homo sapiens* now jump into their definitely-not-jet-skis-but-maybe-canoes and cross the ocean from Asia towards huge new islands in the south, including one that's so big it's actually a continent! Yes, they're about to become the first ever hominins to say …

We used to think only a few humans made the journey, but we now know many thousands migrated to Australia between 65,000 and 50,000 years ago.

"G'DAY, AUSTRALIA!"

> **ACCURACY ALARM** 🚨 BEEEEEEEP!
>
> ## ABORIGINAL AUSTRALIANS
>
> Actually, it wouldn't have been called Australia – that's a modern name. The humans who arrived there around 65,000 years ago gradually formed into hundreds of different cultures, each with its own language, traditions and territory. The descendants of these early adventurers are often called Aboriginal Australians or Torres Strait Islander peoples. Each group's homeland is called a Country. They made beautiful rock art and lived there for tens of thousands of years. However, after 1788, British colonists showed up to grab Australia for themselves. They waged terrible violence against Aboriginal peoples, and the new Australian government passed racist laws that lasted until the 1970s. Remarkably, however, Aboriginal Australians managed to preserve their family histories, songs, languages and art. Their amazing endurance means they can still connect their modern lives back to the Stone Age.

Thank you, Brenna, that's a really important history to know. But we must return to our Stone Age timeline, because I think we might be due for an era upgrade. Hang on to your hats…

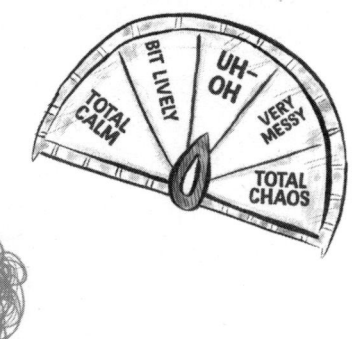

14

INTO THE UPPER PALAEOLITHIC

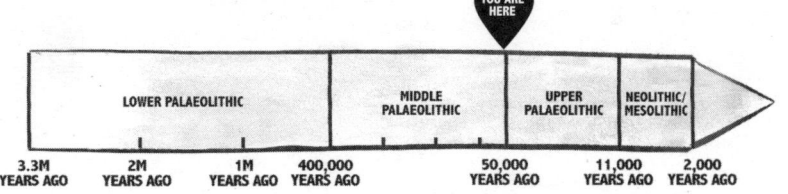

We've cranked the clock forward and instantly crashed into a brand-new era called THE UPPER PALAEOLITHIC – cue the celebratory trumpets! Oh, they haven't been invented yet? Uh … cue the mammoth trumpet noises, then?

TOOOOT TOOOOT!

What do you mean you don't know what the Upper Palaeolithic is?! Oh, all riiiiiiight… Let's do a quick recap. The Stone Age started 3.3 million years ago with the **LOWER PALAEOLITHIC**, then we had the wildly messy **MIDDLE PALAEOLITHIC**. Well, now we're easing our way into the **UPPER PALAEOLITHIC!** Simple, right? And now we're here, let's—

NEW FROM TOOL SHED!

Witness the precision and power of our brand-new technology

INTRODUCING...

MICROLITH

It's the ideal cutting tool for fine detail work. Our expert craftspeople have mastered hitting a large flint core with the exact amount of force needed to ping off a tiny flake ... and make a microlith! Available either in a pointy triangular shape (perfect for your spear!) or as a one-edged scraper.

(Offer only available for *Homo sapiens*. Microlith orders currently only available in Africa. For European delivery times, expect delays of 10,000–20,000 years.)

DON'T BE A FLAKE: GET THE LATEST FLAKE TECHNOLOGY TODAY!

Stupid adverts!!! But yes, *Homo sapiens* have invented a fab new tool tech called microliths. They are smaller and fancier than anything before, and they're certainly very useful, but ... can we please get back to the new era? I want to see all the exciting changes the Upper Palaeolithic has brought!

Microliths were first made by *Homo sapiens* in Africa about 60,000 years ago.

ANOTHER THREE BITE THE DUST

Uh ... actually, I don't see why it's a new era. Nothing much seems to have changed, and— OH NO!

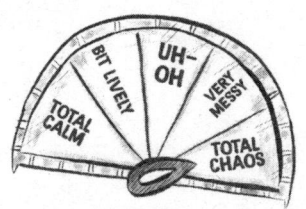

SOUND THE ALARM! WE'VE GOT A TRIPLE EXTINCTION CATASTROPHE!

We've suddenly lost three species of *Homo* at once! That's careless, isn't it?! What happened? Maybe they've succumbed to the pressures of climate change? Or run out of their fave foods? Or caught some terrible disease? Or perhaps they've just been outcompeted by the smarter, more resilient *Homo sapiens*?

We're not sure!

Whatever it is, we must wave bye-bye to *Homo floresiensis*, *Homo luzonensis* (who it feels like we've only just met!) and Denisovans! That leaves just *sapiens* and Neanderthals…

I'd be worried if I were the Neanderthals. I'm not pointing any fingers, but stuff seems to go wrong whenever *sapiens* show up in a new place. Other hominins are being knocked down like skittles.

Then again, humans do make the place look nice! This inventive species has a knack for artistic flair. Obviously they're not the only ones – Neanderthals have been doing cool stuff with colours, patterns and shapes for ages, but it appears that *sapiens* are even artsier. Let's admire their work!

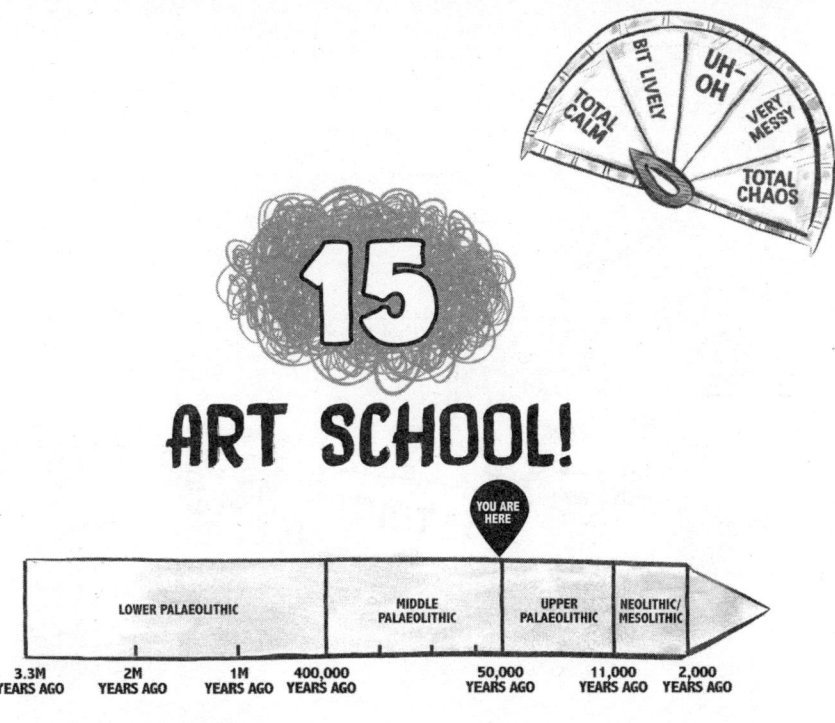

15
ART SCHOOL!

Here in South East Asia, at the start of the Upper Palaeolithic, humans are experimenting with a brand-new form of self-expression: they're painting beautiful portraits of real things on cave walls. And they look AMAZING! An early effort, in Indonesia, shows three half-animal/half-human figures and a wild pig with bristly fur, a round belly, skinny little legs and lumpy warts on its nose. It's such a perfect pig painting – almost a *Pig*casso masterpiece! – you can immediately tell what it is (which is a lot better than anything I can doodle).

> Literally as we were writing this book, scientists announced it's 51,000 years old, making it the oldest artistic representation of a real thing ever discovered. But I bet they'll find even older!

But it's not just in South East Asia where the art scene is exploding – because *Homo sapiens* have finally made it to Europe! This means they're coming face to face with Neanderthals, and having to survive in much tougher Ice Age conditions. And, if they're spending their days hanging out in cold, dark caves, maybe that's the perfect place to practise their art? Perhaps they've even got time to teach useless doodlers like me?! Let's enrol at Stone Age Art School!

Roughly 54,000 years ago! A second group arrived around 45,000 years ago, and then a third about 42,000 years ago.

ART SCHOOL
Welcome to Cave Art 101

YOU WILL NEED
- A cave
- A fire
- Pigments from ground-up rocks (black & red recommended, yellow also good)
- Liquid (wee or animal blood)
- Painting tool (flint scraper, wolf bone or stick)

What to do

Welcome, my darlings, to art school! We shall begin by moistening the pigments with your chosen liquid. Now use your painting tool to smear it onto the cave wall. Don't forget to light your fire. The flames will cast flickering shadows so your painted animals seem to move! Gorgeous work, my lovelies.

Inspiration

Why not let your imagination run wild by showing animals running wild? You could paint deer, goats, ibexes, owls, bison, horses, pigs, woolly rhinoceroses and mammoths, aurochs and whatever else looks good for lunch. Or, if you love horror, perhaps paint the scary animals who want to eat YOU for lunch! There's lions, wolves, panthers and terrifyingly huge cave bears – or why not paint some bonkers animal-human hybrids that are a mixture of both beasts and people?! Unleash your imagination, sweeties!

Techniques

OK, let's talk techniques! You can paint just the outline of animals, or you can shade in their bodies to show the colour of their fur – both approaches are just lovely, darlings. To add extra movement, why not give the animals too many legs? Sure, it looks weird at first, but sometimes the light bouncing between the different sets of legs makes it look like the creature is galloping – delightful! Indeed, the trick works even better if you engrave two slightly different images of the same animal on either side of a disc, put a thread through the centre and then spin it on the string – it looks like the animal is moving! Isn't modern art wondrous?

Tips for beginners

Ah, I see some of you are struggling to capture the graceful movement of the animals. Fear not, darlings! Might I instead suggest bedazzling the wall with your own handprints? It's very easy to achieve – even little kids can do it. Just spray paint around your hands with a paint tube! All you need is a hollow bird bone which you can fill up with paint, and then blow into it to create a splattery stencil effect. And if you're struggling, you can always get a friend to lend you a *hand* … ha ha ha, get it? A HAND?

My talents aren't appreciated here. Class dismissed!

ART ATTACK

There are lots of European caves with Stone Age art in them, but the most famous are Lascaux and Chauvet in France, and Altamira in Spain. So many people have visited Lascaux that the humidity from their breath and sweaty bodies damaged the cave art, so now tourists are banned! Instead they can visit a high-quality replica. We think children may have made the handprints in some caves, as the hands look very small. Scientists are studying how people's brains processed images in the dark caves, and whether the firelight made animal paintings come to life, like an early animation.

All this wonderful art shows how talented these humans are, and how closely they must study animals to be so good at painting them. When I draw a dog it looks like a chubby gopher, but with Stone Age cave art you can really tell the differences between owls, panthers, lions, mammoths and more. These people are clearly fascinated by animals – and maybe for different reasons. Some they eat, some they run away screaming from, and perhaps some they even worship? Who knows!

Most cave art shows animals we hunt. But at Chauvet Cave in France, we see lions and fearsome predators.

ALL KINDS OF ART

It isn't just paintings that artists are creating here in the Upper Palaeolithic era. They also make lovely jewellery from beads, animal claws and teeth; they carve notches into bones to help count the days of the moon's cycle; and they make gorgeous sculptures from soft stone, mammoth ivory and clay. These are small enough to be carried around and passed on to the next generation. A particular favourite design is a figurine of a mother goddess. Artists also seem to love depicting animal-human hybrids that mix together their body parts.

ACCURACY ALARM

FANCY FIGURINES

Oh, don't get me started on those human-animal hybrids, Greg! Stone Age sculptures are fascinating because they show the long history of human creativity – it's intriguing to wonder if they are depicting real people or primitive gods of nature. They also show details of hairstyles and clothing, so we can see what people were wearing 40,000 years ago! The most famous example of an animal-human hybrid is the so-called Lion Man of Hohlenstein-Stadel, found in Germany. It's 31 centimetres tall and a modern artist took 400 hours to make a copy using prehistoric tools, so it's an amazing work of art. However, I get grumpy about it because other experts say it's a mix of lion and human, but I think it's obviously a cave bear standing on its hind legs!

What on earth is that meant to be?

Humans sure do love making art, but Neanderthals are no layabouts either. They're not painting walls, but they do like to paint shells and— HANG ON! WHERE ARE THEY?

OH NO!

WHERE HAVE THE NEANDERTHALS GONE???!!!

It's not good news, Greg...

DON'T TELL ME THEY'VE GONE EXTINCT TOO!!!!!!!!!

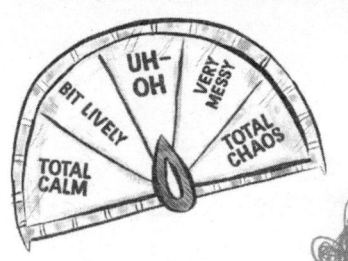

16
SO LONG, NEANDERTHALS!

| LOWER PALAEOLITHIC | MIDDLE PALAEOLITHIC | UPPER PALAEOLITHIC | NEOLITHIC/ MESOLITHIC |

3.3M YEARS AGO — 2M YEARS AGO — 1M YEARS AGO — 400,000 YEARS AGO — 50,000 YEARS AGO — 11,000 YEARS AGO — 2,000 YEARS AGO

YOU ARE HERE

OH NO! THERE GO THE NEANDERTHALS!!!

Do you know what that means? *Homo sapiens* are the Last Ones Standing. All the many other species of hominins we've met in this book are now extinct!

We've not had room to mention them all, but over 20 species!

Hmm, every time *Homo sapiens* spread out to a new place, other hominins already living there quickly die out. Are we the baddies, Brenna?

A small community of Neanderthals possibly survived for longer on the island of Gibraltar, near Spain.

SURVIVAL OF THE FITTEST

I don't think so! I doubt *Homo sapiens* were murdering their rivals. Neanderthals and Denisovans lived in smaller groups — there were maybe a maximum of 50,000 Neanderthals in the whole world. This gave humans better genetic diversity (making them less vulnerable to diseases), and also provided bigger networks of friends and family to rely upon in difficult times. During the Ice Ages, their social skills might have made them better at solving food and shelter problems. However, maybe the other *Homo* species didn't "die out" at all! Humans interbred with them, and their DNA is part of ours today, so perhaps Neanderthals and Denisovans are still right here, inside us!

So, Neanderthals are gone. And unfortunately for the surviving *Homo sapiens*, this latest Ice Age isn't warming up any time soon. But humans are finding new ways to stay alive. In the turbo-chilly tundra of Russia, people have even started piling up chunky mammoth bones to build houses with wood-burning hearths in the middle. Cosy!

A recently discovered house was made from the bones of 60 different mammoths!

No, it's made FROM mammoths, not FOR them!

But some of these humans are clearly tired of their mammoth mansions and the endless snowstorms, because they're heading off on another adventure.

I LIKE TO BE IN AMERICA!

This land bridge over what is now the Bering Sea possibly appeared about 35,000 years ago when sea levels fell.

On the eastern edge of Russia, this bunch of brave explorers have spotted a <u>land bridge</u> that has popped up where the sea used to be. By crossing it, they're about to become the first ever hominins to set foot in <u>North America</u>!

That's where I'm from!

These people are skilled hunter-gatherers, surviving the freezing Ice Age conditions by using weapons topped with beautiful stone arrowheads to hunt the biggest of big beasts — mammoths, bears, rhinoceroses, big cats, giant sloths, bison and loads more!

Hey! Pick on someone your own size!

STRAIT TO THE POINT

Gotta jump in here, Greg, because this is a fiercely debated area of science! We don't know much about these people, because they didn't leave much behind: just a few stone tools, their camps and remains of the animals they hunted. Until very recently, experts said humans crossed the Bering Strait into the Americas about 15,000 years ago, because that's the age of those arrowheads, called Clovis points (named after Clovis in New Mexico, USA, where they were first found). But then we found ancient human footprints which they dated to 23,000 years ago, thanks to tiny plant seeds in the mud – and that means many experts now think humans were already in North America 25,000 years ago! Indeed, one day we might find evidence it was even earlier, and Greg will have to travel to people's houses to correct all the copies of this book with a big red pen!

No thanks Brenna, I've got terrible handwriting. Don't suppose you fancy doing the corrections for me?

Actually, while we're talking about how amazing the science is, maybe you could help me with something else. You see, I'm pretty sure I just heard a dog bark, but I'm sure there aren't any dogs in the Stone Age ... are there?

I have good news, Greg – go get a stick; it's time to play fetch!

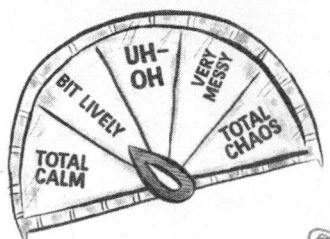

17
WHO'S A GOOD BOY!

For the entirety of the Stone Age, we've heard about animals being hunted by humans, or animals trying to eat humans! But I'm delighted to say we've now got a creature that is helping humans hunt. You might even say it's a cross between a best friend and a useful new tool—

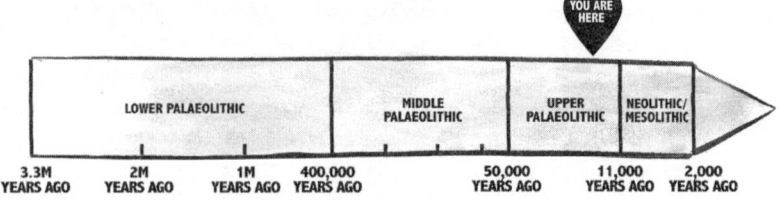

Don't you just hate it when a scary wolf pack attacks your family? Wouldn't you love to have them on your team instead? Now is your chance!

Here at Tool Shed we grabbed a bunch of baby wolves, chose the least aggressive ones, and bred them into a much friendlier animal that we're calling ...

DOG'S NEW FEATURES
- Sharp teeth and powerful legs
- Smaller body, needs less food
- Amazing sense of smell
- Easy to train
- Waggy tail
- All new bark and woof sounds
- Expressive eyes! Cute face! Endlessly loyal!

You'd have to be barking to miss out!

Unlike the vicious wolves you'll find roaming the forests and caves, these dogs are loyal protectors, great hunters and ideal company. They've even evolved to wag their tail, bark and woof, so they can communicate with humans. But that advert said dogs were created by breeding baby wolves – is that true? It doesn't sound very safe!

> Dogs were probably bred all over the world, and then introduced to North America.

I don't think mine is ready yet!

FROM WOLF TO WOOF

Good point, Greg – how did humans tame wolves without being eaten alive? In 1959, a scientist called Dmitri Belyaev set out to answer the mystery. He and his assistant, Lyudmila Trut, took semi-wild silver foxes and kept breeding only the least aggressive cubs. Within a few generations the foxes became friendlier, they liked being stroked, they wagged their tails, their bodies got smaller and their faces became cuter. Amazingly, this experiment is still going and it proves that animals can change very quickly with human interference. We're not sure when dogs first emerged, because wolves and dogs have interbred many times over the past millennia, so the family tree is all tangled up! We have dog bones from 14,200 years ago, but it was possibly as early as 30,000 years ago.

Right! So the new Stone Age dog isn't a cute poodle curled up on a stone sofa, but it's certainly friendlier and more helpful to humans than a snarling dire wolf. They can have a guard dog, a fierce hunter, a trail-sniffing tracker, a sled-pulling husky – and a new best friend!

Well, humans are really starting to figure out how to adapt the wild things around them. And if they can create new animals, maybe they can experiment with other stuff too?

In fact, over in the Middle East, it looks like they're trying some cool new things with plants. Let's check it out!

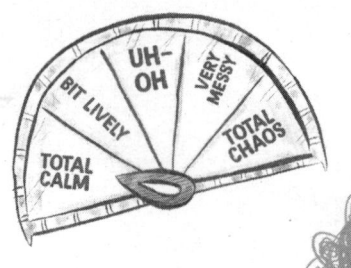

18
THE DAILY GRIND

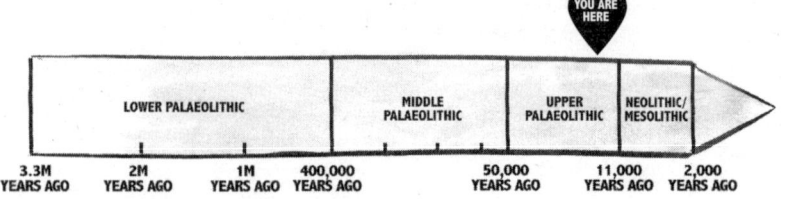

It's been exhausting traipsing all over the place in this book. For several million years, hominins have been constantly on the move. Every species of *Homo* has been a wandering hunter-gatherer – never staying put for long because the weather got bad, or the animals left, or the water dried up, or there was no shelter from the cold. Sure, sometimes they returned to favourite places later, but sticking it out somewhere all year round was unthinkable.

Well, here we are 23,000 years ago, and – amazingly – some people just … uh … thinked it! Yes, a small group of brave souls have chosen a permanent spot to call their home. It's over in the

Not a real word, Greg!

Middle East, in a region called the Levant, on the banks of a freshwater lake. And – unlike the Americas, Europe or northern Asia, which are all in the frozen grip of the Ice Age – this is a lovely place to hang out, with plenty of drinkable water, tons of different animals to eat, lots of nice fishing spots and some great camping locations. In fact, it's such a nice spot, they've started building little brushwood tents to live inside. We might even call them huts! How charming!

We almost never discovered these because the site was underwater for thousands of years.

SERIOUS ABOUT CEREAL

Building cute little huts is not the only thing people are doing differently. They've also become big fans of eating cereal. Yes, every morning they fill their bowls with a tasty helping of cornflak— OOPS! Sorry, that's MY morning routine! No, these Stone Age guys and gals are actually experimenting for the first time ever with messing around with natural crops. They've started taking grass (yes, grass) and grinding it up to eat! Here in the Levant, these humans are particular fans of wild barley, which handily grows near by. The problem is that processing these plants takes loads of effort. Just take a look at this Stone Age cookery channel and you'll see what I mean!

≡ YOU CHEWED!

@YouChewed!   Like Share Save

Barley porridge the natural way

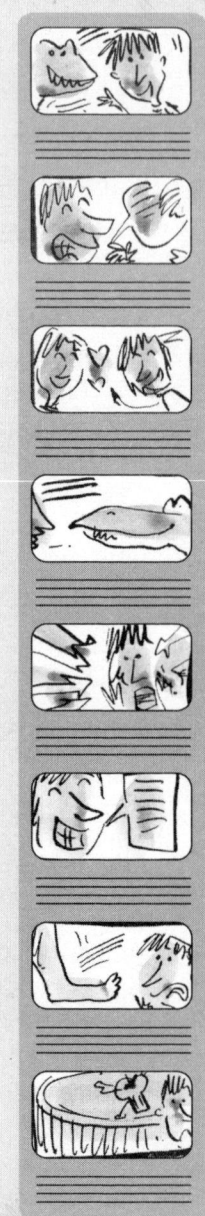

Hey, guys! Welcome to my channel.
I'm Glurk, and today I'm gonna be showing you how to make barley porridge.
Now, I'm sure you've heard it's really difficult, but I think it's totally worth the effort, and we'll take it slow, OK?
So cereals are, like, basically just types of grass. Which is cool and everything, but it makes it, like, really tricky to find them when they grow among loads of other grasses, y'know? Sometimes I'm like, "Mother Nature, could you just *not*, right now?"
Anyway, once you've actually found your barley stalks, with their cute bristly awns, you have to cut them down at the right time of year – like, right before the seeds fall off, you know?

Next up, you need to shake off all the seeds and peel them. Then pound the seed shells with rocks to help release the starchy, good-tasting bit inside. You can use normal rocks, I guess, but my family just got this new invention called a grindstone and it's, like, totally amazing! Smash the seeds up even more to make a paste or powder or whatever, and that's basically, like, uh … your porridge or flour, y'know?

It's a lot of work, and my arm aches from all the grinding, and I've got grindstone grit in my teeth … but apart from that, cereals are great, y'know! Don't forget to like and subscribe for more cookery tips!

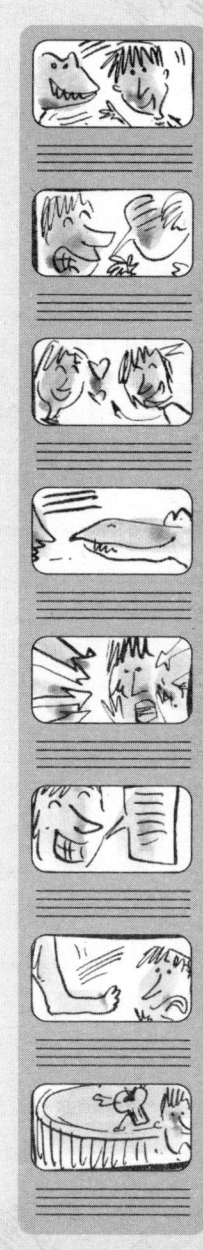

Hmm, even with the help of new grindstones to smash seeds into something edible, this seems like a lot of effort! Why do people bother doing this at all?

ACCURACY ALARM

BARELY BARLEY!

We're not entirely sure! At a site in Israel, called Ohalo II, archaeologists have found hundreds of different plant species in the dirt floors of prehistoric huts. Clearly these people were willing to grind up pretty much anything growing nearby! We think they made a type of porridge, but they probably weren't baking bread yet – our earliest evidence for bread is from 14,500 years ago in Jordan. Some archaeologists have asked if the Ohalo II settlers were maybe starting to brew a gloopy type of barley beer! It might have been a bit early for that, but we've definitely got evidence for beer brewing a few thousand years later.

Ah, that's interesting – making beer takes a lot of time and effort, which suggests humans are becoming skilled enough to think less about basic survival and more about fun stuff, like enjoying a special drink on special occasions. Here's a fun question: are Stone Age humans about to invent parties? I wanna go to a party! Let's see if we can get invited along…

19
PUTTING THE FUN IN FUNERAL

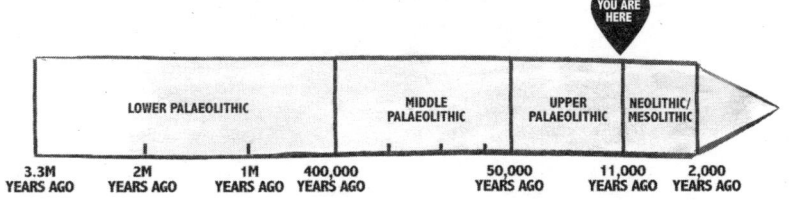

Whoops! I thought we were showing up to a Stone Age party, but we've just walked straight into the middle of a FUNERAL! Yikes, this is awkward.

OK, so it's not the party we were looking for, but the fact these Stone Age people are holding a funeral for someone is important. After all, they usually roll dead people into a ditch or leave them for the birds to eat! But this is a bold new way of saying goodbye.

This particular bunch are busy burying a woman who was around 45 years old. She must have been pretty special during her lifetime because they're chucking all sorts of

> An auroch is a massive cow – they could be 1.8 m tall and were much more aggressive than modern cows!

stuff into the grave with her: bones from an auroch, a leopard, a gazelle, a wild boar and an eagle; two pine marten skulls; a whopping 50 tortoise shells; and – weirdest of all – a human foot! Oh, and now they're piling ten big rocks on top of her body! I wonder who she was to deserve all this unusual treatment?

Is it a bit much?

ACCURACY ALARM · BEEEEEEEP! ·

SPECIAL BURIAL

This lady's body was found at a place called Hilazon Tachtit in Israel. Some archaeologists think she might have been a shaman. In many hunter-gatherer cultures around the world, a shaman is a type of priest and magical healer who can talk to animals and nature. Perhaps that explains all the animal bones? The woman's skeleton shows she was disabled and probably walked with a limp, so maybe the human foot was lobbed into her grave to help her walk better in the afterlife? But we don't know if these people believed in an afterlife, so it's a mystery! Whoever she was, her fancy burial and funeral are proof of how these new communities of settled humans were developing customs.

Talking of customs, here's one I'm a fan of: a big feast! Just look at this excellent funeral catering: newly invented bread, disgustingly gloopy beer and an impressive meat feast buffet – wow, they've cooked three whole aurochs to serve these guests! That's a big barbecue – imagine the biggest cow in the world … and **SUPERSIZE** it into a **MEGA COW!!!** This is basically 300 kilograms of steak being served up. And if you're still hungry, there's also tortoise meat – those poor tortoises! They're either being chucked in a grave or cooked up for lunch…

Worst party ever.

Humans have certainly developed a lot. There are so many changes, in fact, I have a feeling we're about to enter a whole new era…

HELLO, NEOLITHIC ERA!

Are you feeling warm? I'm sweating buckets! At last the huge ice sheets that have covered vast expanses of the planet for the past 65,000 years are melting away, meaning we can say GOODBYE TO THE ICE AGE – see ya! But more than that, it's time to pop on your party hats and explode your party poppers because it's also BYE-BYE TO THE UPPER PALAEOLITHIC ERA …

AND HELLO TO THE

NEOLITHIC ERA!

And hello to the Holocene geological era, which we're still in today!

ACCURACY ALARM

NEOLITHIC/ MESOLITHIC?

Not so fast, Greg! This is really confusing, but it's important. Ready? Neolithic literally means "New Stone"; it was the final phase of the Stone Age, when very big changes arrived. However, it didn't happen everywhere at once. It first showed up in the Levant area of the Middle East we have just been talking about. But, in some parts of the world, the Neolithic took thousands of years to show up, and humans remained stuck in the Upper Palaeolithic, or sometimes in a totally different era called the Mesolithic. Bizarrely, that means two or even three different eras happened at the same time!

THREE AT THE SAME TIME?! And I thought this book couldn't get any more chaotic!

All right, I'll tell you what we should do. Let's look at the fun Neolithic stuff first, and then later on we can get stuck into whatever the heck the Mesolithic is. Deal?

Deal!

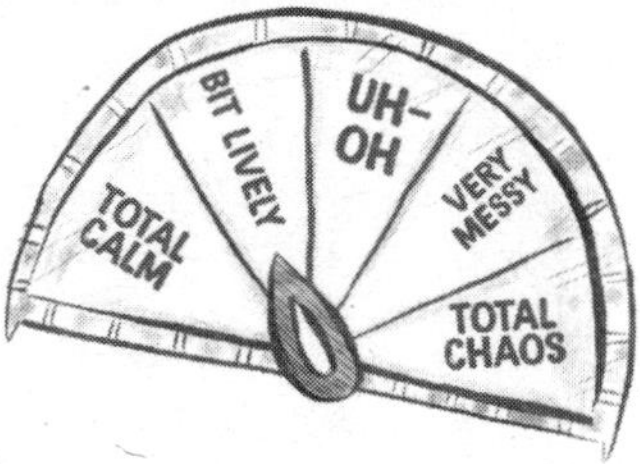

20
BIG BUILDS

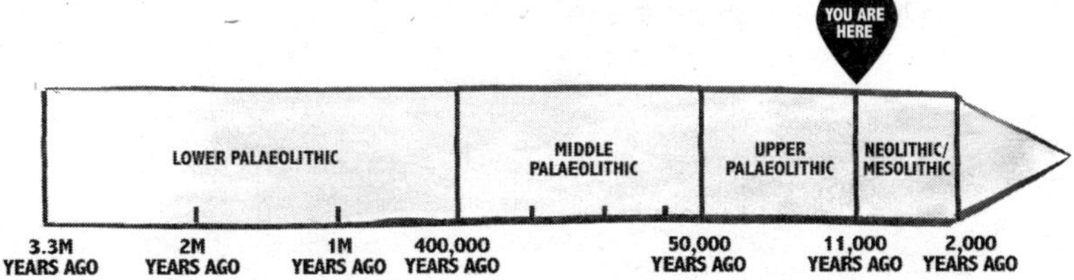

LOWER PALAEOLITHIC | **MIDDLE PALAEOLITHIC** | **UPPER PALAEOLITHIC** | **NEOLITHIC/MESOLITHIC**

3.3M YEARS AGO | 2M YEARS AGO | 1M YEARS AGO | 400,000 YEARS AGO | 50,000 YEARS AGO | 11,000 YEARS AGO | 2,000 YEARS AGO

YOU ARE HERE

OK! New chapter, new era, New Stone Age! We'll kick this Neolithic phase off in style by heading to the mountainous region of West Asia where people are constructing something different from anything we've ever seen before – a huge new project built as a place for lots and lots of people to come together! Previously we've had fabulous houses made of mammoth bones, beautifully decorated caves and sensible brushwood huts, but we've never had something so massive!

← These hills are called the Taş Tepeler or "Stone Hills", and they sit at the bottom of the Taurus mountain range in Türkiye.

In fact, I reckon its construction would make a brilliant episode of a TV property show…

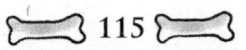

AMAZING BUILDINGS!

Hello and welcome to a new series of *Amazing Buildings*. Today I'm here to meet the team behind a brand-new invention: the world's first stone temple! Let's take a look at the incredible Göbekli Tepe.

Wow, such bold architecture! The aim is to build circular walls made from many small blocks, and then decorate the inner circles with lots of large T-shaped stone sculptures. I love the elegant simplicity of the design!

I'm told by the designers that these stone pillars are meant to be people standing sideways on — how wonderfully imaginative! This temple complex will also be decorated with gorgeous carvings of wild animals, bringing humans and nature together in communal worship.

Of course, a building project of this size can't be done by one person alone. Local volunteers are digging out the heavy limestone rocks, dragging them to the top of the hill and then carefully carving them. It's hard work, but everyone seems raring to get involved — probably because they're being promised regular rewards of beer and meat feasts!

So, don't switch over, because here on *Amazing Buildings* we're about to make history. See you after the break!

THE FIRST TEMPLE

They didn't have TV shows in the Neolithic era, but the rest is true! First discovered in the 1960s, when it was wrongly believed to be a medieval ruin, Göbekli Tepe in south-eastern Türkiye forced us to rethink all our ideas about the Neolithic era!

We used to believe no one could have built large monuments like this before farming was invented, because surely you'd need loads of food to feed all the construction workers. But these temple builders were still hunter-gatherers, who only dabbled in eating wild cereals. The site at Göbekli Tepe is huge – almost as big as 13 football pitches – and sits on top of a 15 metre high tell (a human-made mound of rubble). While several buildings have already been dug up, many more remain buried. We know the site was built on for 1,500 years, but by whom is a mystery. Did it have special caretakers who lived there all year? Or was it only used for special occasions?

PARTY PLACE

Ooh, Göbekli Tepe is totally fascinating! The T-shaped pillars are covered with amazing animal designs, and around the place I can see animal and human skulls with holes drilled into them – maybe to wear as masks?

I'm not sure what it's all for, though. It could be a place for big rituals, or remembering the dead, or charting the changing seasons. Or even just the perfect venue for big summer parties with dancing, feasting and weddings. I dunno, but there are some very large basins for brewing beer, so I reckon people must be having a drink, and then possibly dressing up as animals ... as you do!

So at Göbekli Tepe people are coming together to collaborate on huge projects, and also to have parties! These are massive developments. Stone Age humans' lives are looking more and more like ours. I wonder if there are any more important changes on the horizon?

GROW YOUR OWN!

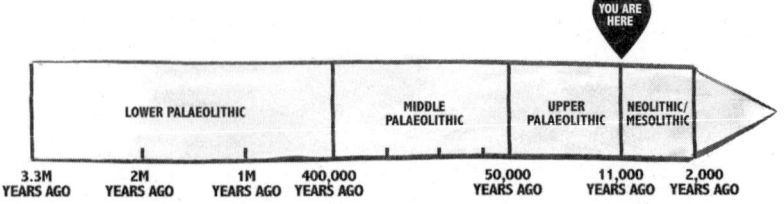

Big news! Remember when people in the Levant started grinding wild cereal grains to make porridge? Well, they've got pretty good at that. So good, in fact, that they've figured it would be easier to plant the seeds themselves, in the places they want them to grow. Convenient, right? Annoyingly, loads of other wild plants keep growing in the same spot and muscling out the nice ones – the big meanies!

To stop that, people have started weeding out the unwanted wild plants, and all that extra space and sunlight means these tasty cereals are starting to evolve. It's taking hundreds and hundreds of years – it's verrrrrrrrrry sloooowwwwwwww – but the seeds are gradually getting fatter and easier to open, and the plants are growing stronger and bigger and easier to harvest, and…

> Archaeologists used to be rubbish at finding tiny Stone Age seeds. But Stuart Struever realized you could chuck buckets of dirt in a bath, and the seeds would float! Much easier to find…

OH MY WORD, THIS IS FARMING!!! HUMANS JUST INVENTED FARMING!!!!

FARMING FRENZY

This is going to change everything! No more wandering! No more waiting around for something to hunt, and no more hunting around for something to gather! Now everybody can stay in one place and work together on one big food-providing field, rather than chasing dinner from watering hole to watering hole. It's genius! I bet this grow-your-own-food idea is going to spread like wildfire through the whole world.

Errr… It's still pretty hard work!

THE SPREAD OF FARMING

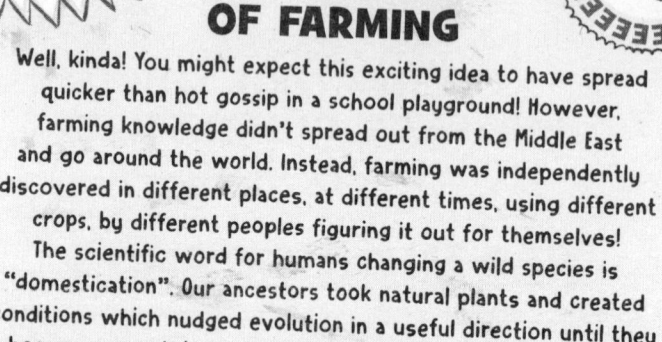

Well, kinda! You might expect this exciting idea to have spread quicker than hot gossip in a school playground! However, farming knowledge didn't spread out from the Middle East and go around the world. Instead, farming was independently discovered in different places, at different times, using different crops, by different peoples figuring it out for themselves! The scientific word for humans changing a wild species is "domestication". Our ancestors took natural plants and created conditions which nudged evolution in a useful direction until they became a new thing: crops! This deliberate growing of food is known as "agriculture". But people in the Neolithic era weren't just changing plants – they domesticated wild animals too!

So farming is being discovered around the world, and there's a delicious buffet to choose from depending on where you go. In the Levant they invent wheat, barley and chickpeas. People in China are growing rice and millet, while in South America they're working on squashes and maize. In different parts of Africa they are focusing on lentils, oil palm and peas, while in India rice is really important.

But as Brenna mentioned, it's not just plants that are now being farmed – it's animals too! We've already seen snarling wolves being domesticated into lovely dogs, but now let's load up our super-addictive farm game and get clicking on some cows!

Welcome to Farm-o-rama, the interactive farming game. To succeed, you'll need to gain experience points (XP) by building your farm, breeding new species of livestock and finding ways to maximize your animals' potential.

BUT WATCH OUT, FARMING CAN BE DANGEROUS!

CLICK TO FOLLOW THE TUTORIAL

STEP 1: SELECT A WILD ANIMAL TO DOMESTICATE

You'll need to grab baby ones to raise on your farm, but watch out for the parents protecting them!

BOAR: Difficulty level 2, XP 2.
These muscular mid-sized beasts taste delicious, but beware their fearsome tusks. Boars can easily kill a human!

BEZOAR IBEX: Difficulty level 1, XP 2.
They're usually not too dangerous, but be careful if they charge at you. These grass-eaters have very long horns.

AUROCH: Difficulty level 3, XP 3.
Huge, muscular cattle. They have horns and a dangerous look in their eyes! They taste great, but they will trample you in a flash…

MOUFLON: Difficulty level 1, XP 2.
Another mid-sized grass-eater. The males have curved horns and can give you a nasty headbutt, but they're pretty safe to approach.

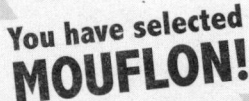

You have selected **MOUFLON!**

STEP 2: BUILD A PEN

If you're going to keep animals, you'll need to actually *keep* them in one place! Build a pen to stop them from wandering off. Nice job! Your baby mouflons are now happily penned in.

STEP 3: DON'T FORGET ABOUT WOLVES!

Oh no! A pack of wolves got into your pen while you were sleeping. Your baby mouflons have all been eaten — you'd better get some more, and train a guard dog to bark if it sees any predators.

STEP 4: FEED YOUR ANIMALS

Feed your mouflons regularly with wild grasses and cereals. They can graze naturally for some of the year, but keep them in the pen for the more dangerous months of winter.

STEP 5: BREED YOUR ANIMALS

Don't let your mouflons breed naturally; pair them up with another friendly farmer's best specimens. You can then gradually get rid of unwanted traits.

STEP 6: NEW SPECIES UNLOCKED!

Congratulations, your selective breeding programme has transformed your mouflons into a new species: the domesticated sheep! It's smaller, less aggressive and pretty happy to stay in one place.

STEP 7: MAKE THE MOST OF YOUR NEW ANIMAL

For maximum XP, shear your sheep and use the wool to make warm clothing. Luckily the wool will grow back. You can also try milking your sheep and drinking it. Don't forget animal poo burns really well as cooking fuel too — a fun bonus! Of course, that leads us to dinner time. If you get hungry, you can always eat your sheep!

STEP 8: BEWARE NEW DISEASES!

Warning! If you cram too many animals into your pen, and then spend your days standing in their poo, getting peed on, touching their mouths, drinking their milk and getting their blood on your hands, then you're going to catch some nasty animal diseases, and they're probably going to catch your nasty human ones! That's the price of having a constant supply of milk, cheese, meat, leather and woolly jumpers at the bottom of your garden...

STEP 9: ADD OTHER ANIMALS TO YOUR FARM

Well done on creating the domesticated sheep. Why not try ibexes, aurochs and boars? If you breed them correctly, you'll soon have a farm filled with goats, cows and pigs!

EXPANSION PACK NOW AVAILABLE!

Grow your farm further and breed fast horses for riding and strong donkeys for carrying stuff. Oh, and don't forget ducks, geese and chickens. These domesticated birds will give you tasty eggs, a different type of meat, and a good chuckle when you watch them waddle (ducks are hilarious!).

That was a fun game! All that farming that the humans are getting good at is introducing new species, slowly turning the animal world into the one we recognize in the modern day. But while humans are busy inventing new animals in West Asia, in other parts of the world quite the opposite is happening. I'm getting all sorts of extinction alerts coming through from the Americas! We'd better go and find out what's causing all the commotion.

We know when goats were domesticated in Türkiye because scientists have found high levels of Stone Age goat wee soaked into the dirt!

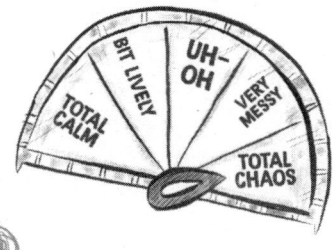

22

THE MYSTERY OF THE MISSING MEGAFAUNA

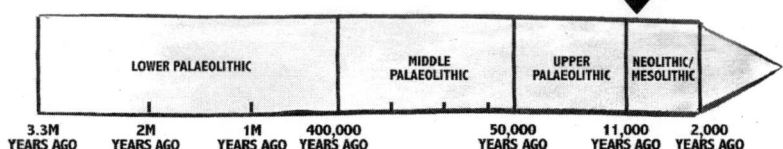

Something's going horribly wrong. It's TOTAL CHAOS again!

The Americas were once filled with a huge assortment of amazing animals, all of them cheerfully unbothered by people. But for the past 15,000 years, humans have been running around the place, chucking their javelins, rocks and sharp Clovis points, jabbing and stabbing with spears and axes, shooting willy-nilly with their bows and arrows, scaring the beasts with their flaming torches ... and, well, suddenly these animals are going extinct alarmingly quickly. Just look at these posters for missing megafauna!

This is the sciencey term for large animals.

Have you seen these missing animals? If found, please return to the wild. APPROACH WITH CAUTION!

AMERICAN CAMEL
(*Camelops*)
Size: 2.2 metres tall
Weight: 800 kilograms
Last seen in North & Central America

Careful, it might kick you!

GIANT ARMADILLO
(*Glyptodon*)
Size: 1.5 metres tall
Weight: 1,800 kilograms
Last seen in South America

Watch out for the spiky club tail!

GIANT GROUND SLOTH
(*Megatherium*)
Size: 3.5 metres tall
Weight: 3,800 kilograms
Last seen in South America

Beware the big claws — and don't let it sit on you!

SABRETOOTH TIGER
(*Smilodon*)
Size: 1 metre tall
Weight: 340 kilograms
Last seen in North America

Fear the long stabby teeth!

DIRE WOLF
(*Aenocyon dirus*)
Size: 1 metre tall
Weight: 65 kilograms
Last seen in North America

Avoid its bone-crunching jaws!

GIANT TERROR BIRD
(*Phorusrhacos*)
Size: 2.4 metres tall
Weight: 130 kilograms
Last seen in South America

Look out for its murderously sharp beak!

COLUMBIAN MAMMOTH
(*Mammuthus columbi*)
Size: 4.2 metres tall
Weight: 10,000 kilograms
Last seen in North & Central America

Careful of the 5-metre tusks!

WOOLLY MAMMOTH
(*Mammuthus primigenius*)
Size: 3.5 metres tall
Weight: 6,000 kilograms
Last seen in North America

Try not to get trampled!

ACCURACY ALARM — **BEEEEEEEP! BEEEEEEEP!**

A BIG GOODBYE

We're not sure why so many megafauna suddenly vanished – probably a mix of climate change and hunting. Occasionally local natural disasters such as drought and wildfires killed loads of animals. Animals also sometimes fell into sticky tar pits, like the one in La Brea (in Los Angeles) which preserved loads of fossilized animals, allowing scientists to study how they evolved! Whatever the cause, around the world, more than a hundred species of large animals went extinct between 50,000 and 10,000 years ago. Africa lost only a few species, hence why safari holidays are so amazing! The Americas were hit much harder, and Australia was worst of all. It lost nearly 90% of its megafauna, including giant kangaroos, giant wombats, giant koalas, and the brilliantly named Demon Duck of Doom – a massive flightless bird that looked like a mix of duck and emu! To be honest, it's probably good it died out – it sounded terrifying!

Not at all, I'm very sweet!

Oops, apologies to animal lovers reading this book; I didn't realize it would get so depressing! Anyway, I think our emergency detour is done. We should probably get back to West Asia, where Neolithic humans are still coming up with exciting new ideas, including one you might find familiar…

23
HOUSE HUNTING IN ÇATALHÖYÜK

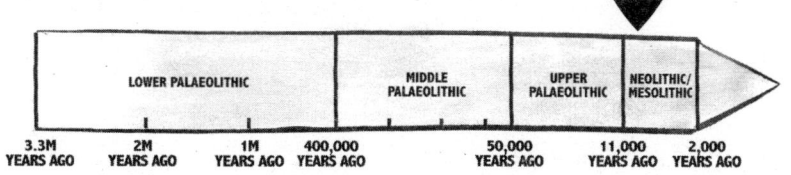

We're in the middle of the shiny new Neolithic era, and although big beasts are dying out, the opposite is happening with humans. Now they've discovered the benefits of staying in one place, the population is suddenly growing. For the last thousand years, tiny hamlets have been popping up in West Asia. But now something even bigger is coming along! People are probably shouting: "LET'S MOVE TO THE BIG VILLAGE!" Oops, sorry, getting ahead of myself. I meant: "LET'S INVENT THE BIG VILLAGE, AND *THEN* MOVE TO IT!"

Çatalhöyük is swiftly becoming the hot new place to live! But big progress can bring big challenges, and the chaos meter is showing a surprising amount of chaos for something as sensible as living in a village. That's because this village looks like no other you've seen before. Let's ask an estate agent to show us around the unusual set-up.

This is the modern Turkish name. We have no idea what Stone Age people called it as they hadn't invented writing yet!

Looking for your dream house? Çatalhöyük is a real up-and-coming area, and streets ahead of the competition ... which is hilarious, really, because we don't have streets, and there is no other competition!

Here we believe in a very cool architectural philosophy you might call cramming-in-as-much-as-possible-without-thinking-it-through. Basically, it's just mudbrick houses in every direction, with no gaps between them, no streets and no front doors! We enter and exit houses through the roof. So by moving here, you're really going up in the world!

Wanna go somewhere? Just climb up onto the top of your house, walk across everybody else's rooftops and climb down – easy! Wanna go to work? Climb two ladders! Wanna get some food? Climb two ladders! Wanna go and YELL AT YOUR ANNOYING NEIGHBOUR BECAUSE THEY KEEP LETTING THEIR GOAT WALK ON YOUR ROOF, AND ALSO THE GOAT KEEPS POOING ON YOUR HEAD?! Climb two ladders!

Do you know what, I don't think I'd like to live here!

INTERIOR DECOR!

OK, it wasn't perfect, but let's cut them some slack. Villages were a brand-new idea – you're always going to have teething problems! Besides, it definitely wasn't all bad. As an archaeologist, I have dug at Çatalhöyük, and it's totally fascinating. You can see how people personalized their walls with decorations, including zigzag patterns in brown and red dye, handprints (just like the ones in much older cave art!), and lots of thrilling images of leopards, bulls, goats, deer and my personal fave: a vulture with human legs! Apparently it was also cool to have bull horns mounted on the walls, because who doesn't love worshipping mighty bulls? Unless they were just used as coat hooks... Who knows!

Sure, that's all very nice, but you're forgetting to mention one unusual design feature: the dead bodies buried under the floor! It's not in every house, but some have the remains of nearly 60 people stashed under the sleeping area! Yikes!

We think sometimes they dug up the bodies, painted faces on the skulls and showed them off!

So, here in the Neolithic, humans are gathering in larger communities than ever before, and building themselves permanent houses next to reliable fields in which to grow reliable food and keep reliable animals. It's all very sensible!

Everything is going swimmingly and— Oh, hang on – what's this?

24

DAIRY BEWARE-Y!

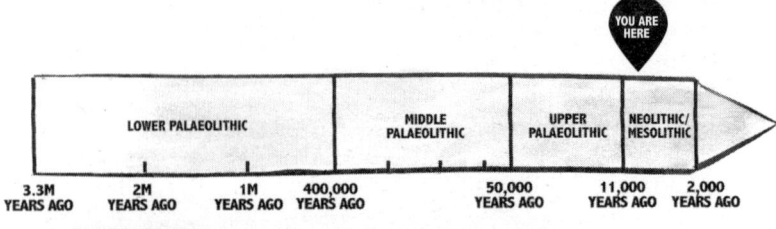

We interrupt this book to issue a safety warning on behalf of Neolithic farmers everywhere.

PLEASE TAKE EXTRA CARE DRINKING ANIMAL MILK!

We are now learning that it makes most people who consume it <u>violently unwell</u>.

Unfortunately, we don't know why this is happening! For some people, milk is lovely, nutritious and delicious! But, weirdly, many milk drinkers are suffering terrible cramps, vomiting, diarrhoea and very bad farts. With apologies on behalf of dairy farmers everywhere...

STAY MILK SAFE!

Huh, that's strange! Why can't Stone Age people drink milk? I enjoyed milk on my cereal this morning, and my tummy feels fine!

MILK MAYHEM

Neolithic people in the Levant and Türkiye started drinking animal milk at least 9,000 years ago. But most mammals can't drink milk after they are babies, and humans were the same – a lot of them would have got very sick slurping a Neolithic milkshake! However, around this time some humans began to evolve a gene that let their stomachs process milk. This gene is now found in about 35% of humans, but it's much more common in certain places: for example, about 89% of people in the UK have it, but in South Asia it's only 20%. Two-thirds of the world's population are lactose intolerant (what we call not being able to drink milk), so milk drinking is actually pretty weird!

Ah, so many people wouldn't dare to drink scary dairy! But, luckily, Neolithic people have also learned that turning milk into cheese and yoghurt makes it easier to digest, so they can still get some extra benefits from their farm animals!

FORWARDS AND BACKWARDS

Now we've got that health warning out the way, let's continue. We've been seeing a lot of change as we hurtle through the Neolithic era – new villages, new animals, new crops, new temples and even new food allergies! But remember what I said earlier about this change not happening everywhere at once?

We've been enjoying all the excitement in West Asia. Meanwhile, over in western Europe, things are not quite as glamorous. Here they're still going through the Mesolithic era, with none of the perks of the Neolithic. In fact, if we head over to Britain, we'll be going forward in time, but it might feel like we're actually going backwards...

The ice had melted, but Mesolithic people were still stuck in their old habits.

25

BACK IN BRITAIN

Welcome to the Mesolithic!

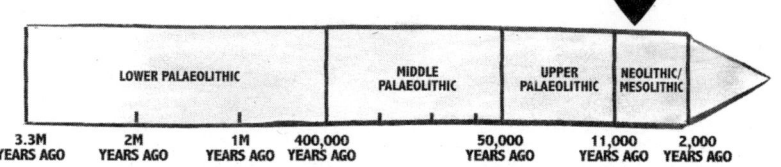

Welcome to Britain, where things aren't quite so thrilling. Nobody's farming crops, or guzzling milk, or domesticating animals, or living in villages ... nope, they're all still traditional hunter-gatherers over here. It's all a little bit ... backwards?

In fact, the only reason to visit is that it's easy to get to: unlike modern-day Britain, it's connected to mainland Europe by <u>a land bridge</u>. Apart from that, I'm finding this all a bit of a let-down, to be honest. What have they been doing over here in Britain, while we were with the impressive builders in Neolithic West Asia?

The bridge is called Doggerland.

CHEDDAR MAN

While Neolithic farmers in Türkiye made big leaps forward, the islands of Britain and Ireland were still home to hunter-gatherers. The most famous of these people is known as Cheddar Man: he lived 10,000 years ago, and his bones were found in Gough's Cave in Cheddar, Somerset. In 2018, scientists examined his DNA and found he had dark skin, dark curly hair and blue eyes – which is probably what most Mesolithic Europeans looked like. Gough's Cave is also famous because 14,700 years ago it was home to cannibals, who ate other people and turned human skulls into drinking cups, and made weird zigzag markings on their bones!

Yikes! More cannibalism?! I thought we'd left that behind! Phew, I'm glad we weren't here for that bit... Still, it's not totally boring here now. Let's head further north, where there are some exciting things to see.

STAR ATTRACTION

This is Star Carr, in Yorkshire, where archaeologists found the oldest ever house in Britain.

OK, so no one is building full villages yet, but they do seem to be pretty good at carpentry. Here we are at an impressive hunting camp with circular wooden huts where people can stay for months at a time, which is a definite upgrade on constantly wandering around, chasing animals all year.

Oh, and just like the beer-drinking revellers at Göbekli Tepe, these Mesolithic Britons really love dressing up as animals – just look at these awesome stag antler masks! If they've invented parties, it can't be so bad here.

It really feels like it's only a matter of time before this bunch of backwards Britons get the memo from western Asia, and ditch their Mesolithic ways. Surely all the newest Neolithic novelties will soon cross that lovely land bridge and—

OH NO! Where did the land bridge go??? Urgh, typical! Well, that's going to delay the big Neolithic switch-over, isn't it? Hmm, you know what? My book, my rules – let's just jump ahead 2,000 years... WHOOOOOOOOOSHH!

Ice Age glaciers had completely melted by 8,000 years ago, causing sea levels to rise. That's how we got the English Channel!

WELCOME TO THE NEOLITHIC ERA ... AGAIN!

That's better! Here we are 6,000 years ago, and let's have a quick look to see what's changed. OH, YIKES! UH... It's a massive change!

Those European farmers finally crossed the Channel, and they've totally replaced the population of Britain! How did that happen?! Did they accidentally bring lethal diseases with them, and the locals weren't immune? Did they run around killing everyone and steal their land? Or did they just show up in such huge numbers that the locals were totally outnumbered? I genuinely don't know! Whatever it was, 99% of the population has been replaced very quickly, which is SHOCKING!

DNA science shows 99% of people in Neolithic Britain were recently descended from southern European farmers – the Mesolithic Britons had vanished!

Well, however it happened, those new people have brought over the new Neolithic ways of doing things, like farming and new tools—

NEW FROM **TOOL SHED!**

Need to chop down big trees so you can dig new fields to plant new crops?

Introducing the all-new *ADZE*! Part axe, part hoe, it's a versatile wonder gadget ideal for log chopping, carpentry and digging. With its smooth stone head and a choice of wooden handles, the adze is the future of farming and forestry.

Get one today, because all the time you'll save soon adze up!

GAH, NOT AGAIN!!! I thought we'd seen the last of these pop-up adverts, but I must admit, it is *quite* funny that we've got ads for an adze! Also, it's a great example of the new Neolithic stuff being brought to Britain. Another exciting thing popping up all over the place is big stone monuments, a bit like what we saw at Göbekli Tepe. Let's find out more!

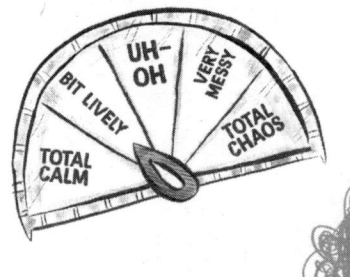

26
MEGA MEGALITHS

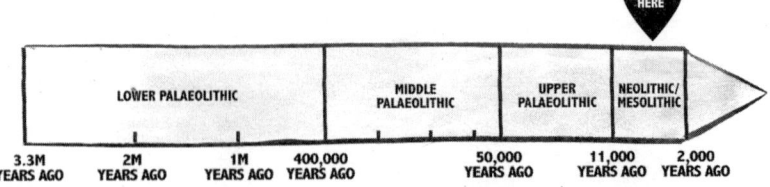

Now we're finally in a new era, we've got loads of new monuments being built in the British Isles, and plenty seem to share a recurring theme: death! They're often burial places for important people, or important families. Not everyone gets a snazzy monument, of course. Ordinary people are probably getting chucked in the nearest river, left for the birds or cremated.

Neolithic burials were often for men in the same family. We don't know what made these men different – were they shamans? Leaders? Relatives?

But other monuments are also about connecting living people to their landscape, to each other and to the sun, moon and seasons. We should probably give all these monuments a name… We've had microliths before,

146

which were tiny sharp flakes used as slicing tools. Well, now it's time for the opposite: not microliths, but ...

MEGALITHS: VERY. BIG. STONES!

← They can also be made of earth.

Yes, the farmers from southern Europe who have turned up in Britain have plenty of building experience, having already erected loads of megaliths along the Atlantic coastline of western Europe, from sunny southern Spain to snowy Sweden! But it's here in the British Isles, and especially on the islands of Ireland and Orkney, that they're doing their finest work. They're putting up standing stones, burial chambers and much more.

So, what do these megaliths look like, and how do we tell them apart? Here's a handy guide!

SPOTTER'S GUIDE TO THE MEGALITHS OF BRITAIN AND IRELAND

MENHIR
A tall standing stone, sometimes erected on its own, sometimes alongside loads of others.

DOLMEN
A simple burial tomb: two or three stones prop up a massively heavy capstone, which sometimes looks like it's magically floating! Ireland's Poulnabrone dolmen is a famous example.

CAIRN
A pile of small stones, very common in Ireland and Scotland. Sometimes huge round mounds; sometimes narrow stacks like Neolithic Jenga!

LONG BARROW
A huge tomb with burial chambers, and soil piled over the top. West Kennet in England is 100 metres long and contained the bones of 36 people who died within 50 years of one another.

CURSUS
A long, narrow avenue with ditches or banks at the sides and ends. Very common in England, they often connected important places to nearby rivers.

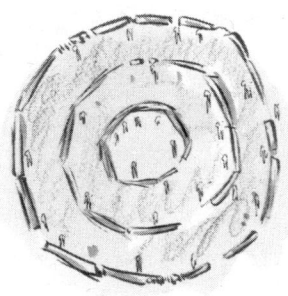

CAUSEWAYED ENCLOSURE
A ring of circular ditches and banks, with small gaps for people and animals to enter. A hang-out for occasional parties, often built on top of hills.

CHAMBERED CAIRN
Like a long barrow, but covered in small stones. Two amazing examples are found at Newgrange in Ireland and Maeshowe on the island of Orkney.

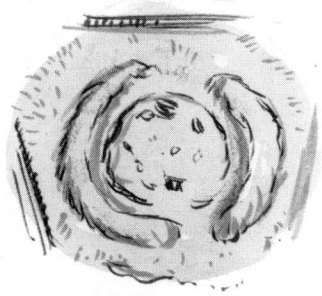

HENGE
Not a stone circle! Actually, the henge is what surrounds a stone circle: circular areas with a raised bank on the outside, then a shallow ditch inside that.

PALISADED ENCLOSURE
A circular area walled off by tall wooden fences called palisades.

With all that heavy stone and soil to move around, megaliths are seriously hard work to construct! They seem to be special places for remembering the dead, gathering people together and celebrating the changing seasons. They're definitely built to last, but why are they plonked where they are, Brenna?

ACCURACY ALARM

BEEEEEEEP! • BEEEEEEEP!

MYSTERIES OF THE MEGALITHS

Some megaliths were built where the old Ice Age glaciers left giant chunks of rock lying around (called glacial erratics — literally a cool name!). Others were built in line with the movement of the sun and stars. For example, the chambered cairns at Newgrange and Maeshowe are famous for facing the sunrise, so that during winter — and particularly on the winter solstice on 21 or 22 December, when the sun is at its lowest in the sky — the sun's rays shine directly into their passageways, filling it with beautiful light. It takes some serious planning to pull that off!

People in the Neolithic sure love building massive monuments out of stone. And what else can they make from stone? HOW ABOUT EVERYTHING!!!

27
SKARA BRAE

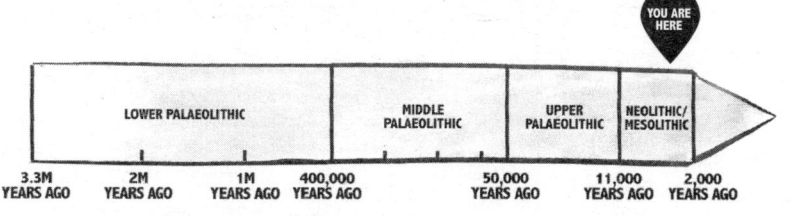

If we're talking about things made of stone, you might be expecting us to go and check out the super-famous Stonehenge monument, right? Actually, the most interesting project happening right now is up on the island of <u>Orkney</u>. Here people are ⟵ *Off the northern coast of mainland Scotland.* building an amazingly impressive complex of interconnected monuments, including ten adorably cosy stone houses covered in grassy mounds.

And what do you reckon their furniture is made of? STONE, OF COURSE! Imagine that furniture catalogue…

Introducing the luxury furniture range from

HOMES OF STONE!

 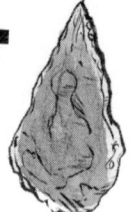

We've got all your must-haves for modern Stone Age living...

Want practical shelving to display your favourite trinkets? Carve them from stone for ultimate shelf strength!

SO STONY!

Come on down to Homes of Stone to see our collection

Need to keep your seafood and fishing bait in wet tanks? Stone is waterproof AND unbreakable: those limpets will never escape!

Looking for somewhere comfy to rest after a long day? Try our stone beds! They're the firmest mattress Mother Nature can provide: ideal for anyone with a bad back.

– you'll be a-*stone*-ished by the quality!

Huh, so everything at Skara Brae is made of stone — I guess because it's the *Stone* Age?

STONE ALONE

No! There are basically no trees growing near by, so Skara Brae is stone, stone, stone a gogo! The use of stone for everything — even beds! — is one of the things that makes Skara Brae unique. The other thing is how well connected it was. Today we might think of the islands off the coast of Scotland as being very remote, but in the past they hosted busy villages, and people travelled a lot. We wouldn't even have known about these stone houses were it not for a gigantic storm in 1850 that washed the soil away and revealed the buried walls — a visitor immediately called for an archaeologist!

LIFE AT SKARA BRAE

It's not quite the noisy hurly-burly of Çatalhöyük, but there's still lots going on up here. People raise cows, sheep and pigs but they still hunt wild deer and boar, so it's halfway between Neolithic farming and hunter-gathering. They trap fish too, as well as catching them one at a time on a hook, as they live by a freshwater loch. They also trade with and travel between other islands, and sometimes import rarer items from far away, including special stones like haematite.

Skara Brae was home to maybe 50-100 people, and used for 700 years.

And it's not just Skara Brae up here. There's also Barnhouse village with its small round houses, and near by is Maeshowe chambered cairn with its incredible solar alignment so the sun shines through the passageway during winter. There's also the standing stones of Stenness, so there's plenty to see around here!

ACCURACY ALARM

NESS OF BRODGAR

BEEEEEEEP! BEEEEEEP!

The archaeology on Orkney is very exciting, and there's lots of stuff to see if you ever visit. A few centuries after the standing stones of Stenness were built, another huge circle made from 60 stones called the Ring of Brodgar was constructed. What's even more impressive is a massive complex called the Ness of Brodgar, first discovered in 2003. This was built on a thin strip of land between two lochs. It contains many buildings with tiled roofs, colourful walls and decorative art inside. This shows us that loads of people gathered in Orkney to feast, share ideas, pick people to marry and mark the changing seasons. It's possible people travelled hundreds of miles for these parties!

Talking of party places, we've got one more stop on our whirlwind Stone Age tour. In fact, we mentioned it at the very start of the book. At long last, twenty-seven chapters later, it's time to finally discover the story of Stonehenge!

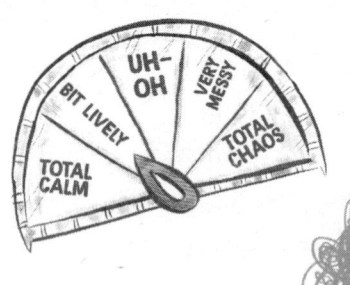

28
SECRETS OF STONEHENGE

	LOWER PALAEOLITHIC			MIDDLE PALAEOLITHIC	UPPER PALAEOLITHIC	NEOLITHIC/ MESOLITHIC
3.3M YEARS AGO	2M YEARS AGO	1M YEARS AGO	400,000 YEARS AGO	50,000 YEARS AGO	11,000 YEARS AGO	2,000 YEARS AGO

YOU ARE HERE

Here we are 5,000 years ago, standing on an almost <u>treeless grassy plain</u>. One day, this is going to be one of the most famous sites in the world, but for now there's nothing spectacular to

Salisbury Plain in Wiltshire, England.

Where's Ug?

see. In the past 500 years, people have been building simple monuments here. But now they're hard at work on a much bigger project. It starts with a causewayed enclosure, 100 metres wide, which connects to a cursus avenue running all the way to a long barrow tomb. Then they dig a circular ditch and pile up the soil into an outer bank. It's a lot of sweaty work, swinging their adzes and moving all that heavy earth. Oh, but they're not done yet…

Next up, they dig <u>56 holes</u> around the inner edge of the circle, and in some of these they bury the remains of dead people, some of whom grew up in west Wales – 150 miles away!

These Aubrey Holes were found in 1666 and named after the keen historian who dug them up!

> OI, GREG! IT'S CALLED STONEHENGE, NOT HOLEHENGE! WHERE ARE THE STONES?!

Oh sorry! Yes, let's get cracking on building our famous monument. Luckily henges are SO popular in the Neolithic, I've even found a DIY instruction kit!

> DOWN HERE!

MY FIRST DIY STONEHENGE KIT

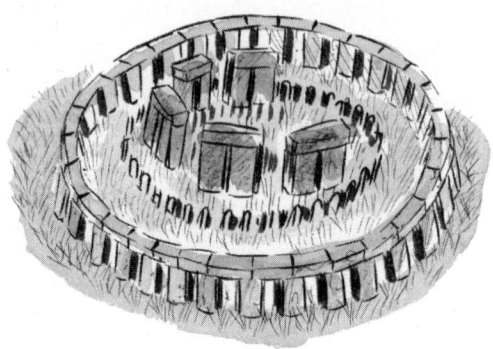

Follow these simple instructions to make your henge:

1. Got your circle of holes dug? Great! Insert your stones – you'll need pre-used stone circle pieces dragged all the way from west Wales. They're really pretty, and they only weigh 4 tonnes, so it's totally worth it!

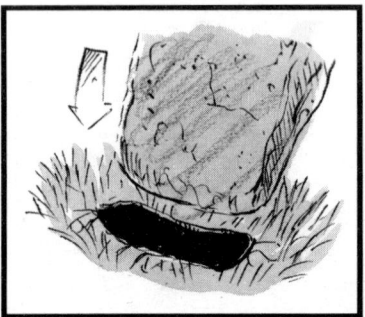

2. Don't rush the design! Spend 200 to 300 years rearranging your stones, or build a second henge. If you don't like it, you can always change it back.

3. Supersize your henge with some massive squared off sarsen stones! Each weighs about 25 tonnes, but luckily we stock these locally. Use ropes and strong logs to haul, roll, hoist, drag and yank 80 sarsens to your henge. You might need some friends to help.

4. Time to get serious about decoration. Try a trilithon: two upright stones and a third lintel laying across the top.

WARNING!
DON'T STAND UNDER A LINTEL WHEN IT'S BEING HOISTED UP – DANGER OF CRUSHING!

5. Don't forget to carve sticky-out pegs into the top of your pillars and then drill matching holes in the underside of the lintels. The joints will lock snugly together and stop the lintel falling off.

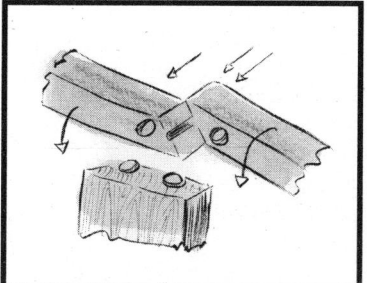

6. Make sure your trilithons are in the right spot to line up with the sun on the winter and summer solstices – they're a nightmare to move if you get it wrong!

7. Got spare stones rattling around? Better set them up too! Put a ring of 30 stones outside your circle of trilithons. Again, ensure the sun shines through the gaps perfectly, otherwise your seasonal solstice party will be RUINED.

8. Pop a low flat altar stone, a bit like a table, right in the middle of your circle. This might be handy for religious rituals.

Congratulations on your lovely henge – we hope you enjoy many wonderful solstice parties!

The technical term is mortice and tenon joints. ↘

Pretty impressive, hey? Especially how the pieces are locked together by <u>hole and peg joints</u> that you normally see in carpentry or Lego bricks, not prehistoric stonework! It just shows how sophisticated Stonehenge is. And, of course, it took a ton of effort to build … thousands of tonnes, in fact!

ACCURACY ALARM — STONEHENGE'S STONES

BEEEEEEEP! • BEEEEEEEP! •

Yep, never mind building it, just gathering the materials was an incredible effort! Some stones were borrowed from an earlier stone circle in Wales and the 6-tonne altar stone was probably from Scotland!

The larger sarsens are from the Marlborough Downs, only about 15 miles away. That said, I wouldn't want to drag 25-tonne stones even 15 metres!

Stonehenge now has 83 stones, but many are missing from its original design. However, we're lucky to have what we do: only a mile away is Bluestonehenge – all of its stones are gone, and all that's left are the holes!

But the big secret of Stonehenge is this: technically a henge is a circle with a ditch surrounded by a bank of soil. Stonehenge doesn't have this, so it's not ACTUALLY a proper henge … but it's the most famous one in the world!

MORE THAN A HENGE

Well, isn't Stonehenge looking magnificent? But it's not a solo act! It's part of something much bigger. If we wander down this avenue, we can reach the River Avon, and various other important monuments. We can walk between Stonehenge, the Cursus, the smaller stone circle at Bluestonehenge, timber circles at Woodhenge, and a massive earthwork henge at the village of Durrington Walls. This whole area is connected, with Stonehenge as a key focal point. And it's a great place to hang out: people here are enjoying huge BBQ feasts of animals brought from all over the British Isles!

We know of other barrows, cemeteries and monuments in the area – there may be more discoveries to come.

Yes, Stonehenge is only one part of a much larger ritual landscape. In fact, it isn't even the biggest construction project in the area – the nearby Avebury stone circle and the massive mound of Silbury Hill are even mightier monuments!

It's taken ages, but these amazing engineering projects tell us the people in the British Isles are finally getting the hang of the Neolithic era, and— Hang on, why is the chaos meter going haywire?!

UH-OH! I think we have visitors!

29
THE BRONZE AGE

They were originally from the steppe region of eastern Europe and Asia.

Look out – we've landed in total chaos again! And it's all because a bunch of <u>new people</u> just showed up in Britain, and I don't know if they're friendly. There's a lot of them, and some of them have this brand-new blonde hair colour and pale skin. Who are these mysterious new arrivals?

Well, they've brought their own style of bell-shaped pottery beakers decorated with wiggly lines. In fact, they even love to be buried with them when they die. So let's call them <u>the Beaker people!</u>

I guess it's better than being called the potty people!

Yep, that's what scientists actually call them!

But, er, there *are* rather a lot of them. And last time this happened, the new arrivals wiped out the population of Britain! Should we be worried, Brenna?!

ACCURACY ALARM — **BEEEEEEEP! BEEEEEEEP!**

THE AMESBURY ARCHER

Kind of! We're not sure if the Beaker people violently conquered the British Isles, or if they peacefully mixed with the darker-haired locals. What we do know is that over 400 years, the Beaker people gradually replaced 90% of Britain and Ireland's ancient DNA! A famous example of these new arrivals is the Amesbury Archer. He was buried near Stonehenge, and his grave had arrowheads inside. Journalists called him the "King of Stonehenge" because he had the most lavish burial ever found in prehistoric Britain, with 100 beautiful objects beside him, including the earliest ever gold found in the UK. He was obviously important, but scientific tests show the Amesbury Archer grew up in the Swiss Alps! One of the biggest questions is how these people from so far away took over the British Isles.

Uh ... yes, about that... While we've been focused on stone in Britain, the rest of the world hasn't stood still. Remember, change doesn't happen everywhere at the same time! And big changes have been happening elsewhere, as we can tell from the strange, shiny new weapons the Beaker people are carrying. They're like nothing we've seen before! Because in the Middle East and Europe, people have mastered a new material—

TIRED OF STONE AND WOOD?

AARGH, NOT AGAIN!

Setting your sights on something shiny and sharp? Welcome to the greatest tech upgrade since humans discovered fire...

METAL!

Here at Tool Shed we've invented a cutting-edge material with a wicked cutting edge – and we call it BRONZE! It's perfect for making axes, adzes, brooches, armoured breastplates and a brand-new weapon we call a *sword*. So don't get left behind: join the Bronze Age today!

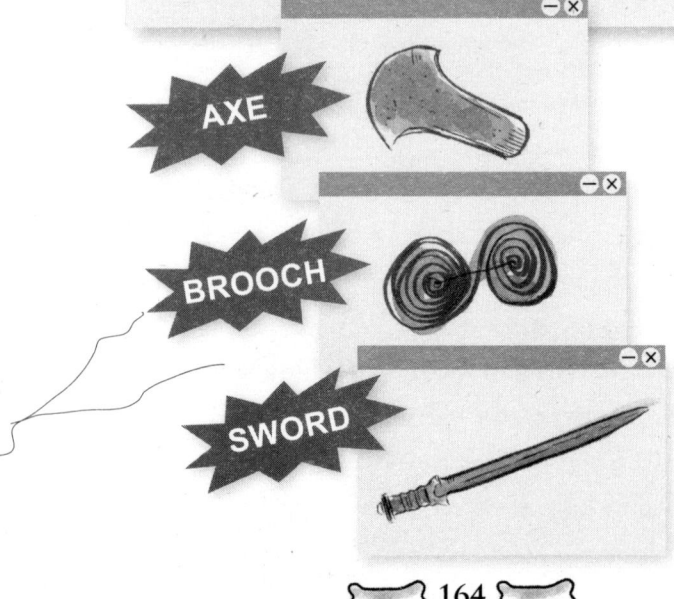

AXE

BROOCH

SWORD

THE END OF AN ERA

WOW!!! Bronze has arrived in Britain – how exciting! It's a mixture of tin and copper, <u>smelted</u> over an extra-hot furnace. And it's a massive tech upgrade, because molten bronze can be poured into a hollow clay or wax mould and made into different shapes. When the bronze cools and hardens, you're left with a strong, sharp and shiny sword or tool or whatever you want!

That means heating and melting.

And if you think this is going to change everything – you're right! Because this means the end of the Stone Age and the start of the Bronze Age. FANFARE, PLEASE!

Actually, the Bronze Age has already started! These Britons are hundreds of years behind places like Egypt and Mesopotamia.

We've done it: we've raced through 3.3 million years of Stone Age chaos. Hooray! No more Palaeolithic puzzles or archaeological mysteries, we're now into the historical period where people actually write stuff down. I KNOW THIS BIT! At last I can launch into my big lecture about—

Oh, the book is finished.

BUM!!!

It's for the best, Greg; my nerves can't handle another one of those annoying pop-up ads!

30
HOW DO ARCHAEOLOGISTS KNOW STUFF?

Before we finish, there's one more mystery we need to solve. We've covered so much stuff in this book, and it was all from AGES ago. Normally, historians like me can study what people in the past wrote down, or the stuff they left behind, to find out what their life was like. The trouble with the Stone Age is it was SO long ago, nobody could write and leave us helpful records. And even when Stone Age people did leave stuff behind, it was usually hard to understand, like random rocks! So how do we know what we know? And why do we keep changing our minds about what was going on with all those ancient hominins?

WHO'S WHO

All through this book we've talked about archaeologists – people who dig up stuff from the past. But actually, there's loads of different jobs with specialist skills that help us piece together the puzzle of the Stone Age. An easy way of spotting these jobs is if their name starts with "archaeo": that means they study old stuff that humans – our ancestors – left behind.

"Archaeo" is ancient Greek for old.

Some experts examine ancient DNA (genetic archaeologists); some study bones from early humans (biological anthropologists); others look at the bones of ancient animals (zooarchaeologists); some test types of soils and rocks, examine ancient weather or changing sea levels (geoarchaeologists); and some look at prehistoric plants (archaeobotanists). You can even have archaeological scientists who do physics and chemistry to find out the ages of things, or experimental archaeologists who try to recreate prehistoric tools, art and even houses and landscapes. Then there are the field archaeologists who get their hands dirty digging trenches, exploring caves, patiently brushing and trowelling, and carefully measuring and photographing whatever they find, before spending years trying to make sense of it. All of these experts help to work out incredible details about Stone Age life, from what the weather was like to what people ate.

Of course, archaeologists are scientists, and scientists love to passionately disagree about how to interpret evidence. But when they combine their amazing talents, that's when very cool stuff happens. It can mean that entire books need to be rewritten – which is very annoying – but it can also mean brand-new species get discovered!

DUNNO? DNA!

One of the coolest technologies that has come along in recent years is sequencing prehistoric DNA. This is when scientists can take ancient hominin DNA and work out information from it. We've mentioned it a few times in this book, because it has been a total game changer for scientists studying our human origins. It has exploded old ideas, told us that humans and Neanderthals had kids together, and revealed the existence of *Homo denisova*. In fact, it's so important that the scientist who pioneered it, Svante Pääbo, won the 2022 Nobel Prize – that's the top award in all of science!

But, Brenna ... uh ... what actually is DNA?

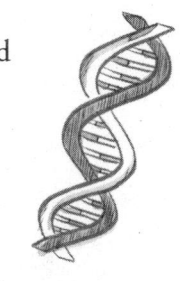

ACCURACY ALARM
PUTTING THE DNA INTO D(E)N(ISOV)A!

BEEEEEEEP! BEEEEEEP!

DNA is a super-tiny chemical which sits in the centre of all living cells and provides the instruction manual for life. Under a powerful microscope you can see it has a double helix shape, like a twisty-turny rope ladder. DNA is made up of four different chemicals labelled A, G, C and T. All living things have just these four letters, which means you and I share 60% of our DNA with bananas ... but you're not a banana, are you, Greg? That's because it's the order of those four letters that matters – even a small reordering makes a huge difference. We share nearly 99% of our DNA with chimpanzees, but we look pretty different! Scientists only discovered the species *Homo denisova* existed when they read the DNA of their bones and realized it was slightly different from our DNA, but also from Neanderthal DNA. So exciting! Unfortunately, DNA doesn't survive very well for earlier species.

Wow! Who knows what else DNA will help us discover about the Stone Age? There's no time to find out now, though – it's time for us to wrap this chaotic journey up!

CHAOS = COMPLETE!

That's the end of our top-speed journey through prehistory – sorry if it got a bit messy along the way! But that's the exciting thing about studying the Stone Age: it lasted millions of years and was filled with jaw-droppingly weird stuff, chaotic weather, dangerous beasts, new inventions and never-ending change. It's the story of how humans adapted to difficult challenges, which sadly our species may yet face again with the climate change crisis … unless we sort ourselves out.

And while the Stone Age was a time of great change, our knowledge of it keeps changing too – new scientific techniques are revolutionizing the study of the prehistoric past in a way that basically melted my brain! Did you know there were FIVE separate times when new discoveries forced us to rewrite the chapters you just read? That's never happened to me before, and this is my seventh book!

That speed of change is totally astonishing, particularly when we're talking about things that happened so very long ago. But it's a wonderful example of how scientists and historians update their ideas when new evidence comes along. That's a great lesson for life – always be open-minded! Maybe one day you'll become an expert researcher too, and you can disprove something you read in this book. That would be awesome!

Until then, thanks for spending time with Brenna and me – you can now go about your daily life knowing that many people have a tiny bit of Neanderthal DNA inside them, dogs used to be wolves, and not everyone can drink milk. And remember that, at any moment, life can suddenly get …

MEET THE MAKERS

GREG JENNER is a public historian, author and broadcaster. He is best known for hosting the BBC's educational comedy podcasts *You're Dead to Me* and *Homeschool History*. As Historical Consultant to CBBC's BAFTA and Emmy award-winning TV comedy series "Horrible Histories", Greg was in charge of all the history facts for 1,500 side-splitting sketches and songs, and the spin-off movie. He has written three books for adults, and released his first children's book, *You Are History*, in 2022. Discover more at **gregjenner.com**

RIKIN PAREKH studied art at Camberwell College of Arts and the University of Westminster. When he's not drawing you'll probably find him at the cinema or at Comic Con. You can see more about Rikin at **rikinparekh.com**

MEET THE ARCHAEOLOGIST

DR BRENNA HASSETT is an archaeologist and anthropologist, and author of two books. She is a lecturer at the University of Lancashire and also works on archaeological digs in places like Greece, Türkiye and Egypt.

My job takes me around the world digging up very old things (like Çatalhöyük), kinda old things (like the people who built the pyramids in Egypt) and not-that-old things (like Victorian terraced houses). I have a PhD in Dental Anthropology – yes, that's a real thing – because my specialism is teeth, but what I really love to study is how humans have changed over time. I also love to write, and have two books that have way less interesting illustrations than this one.

Check out more TOTALLY CHAOTIC adventures ...

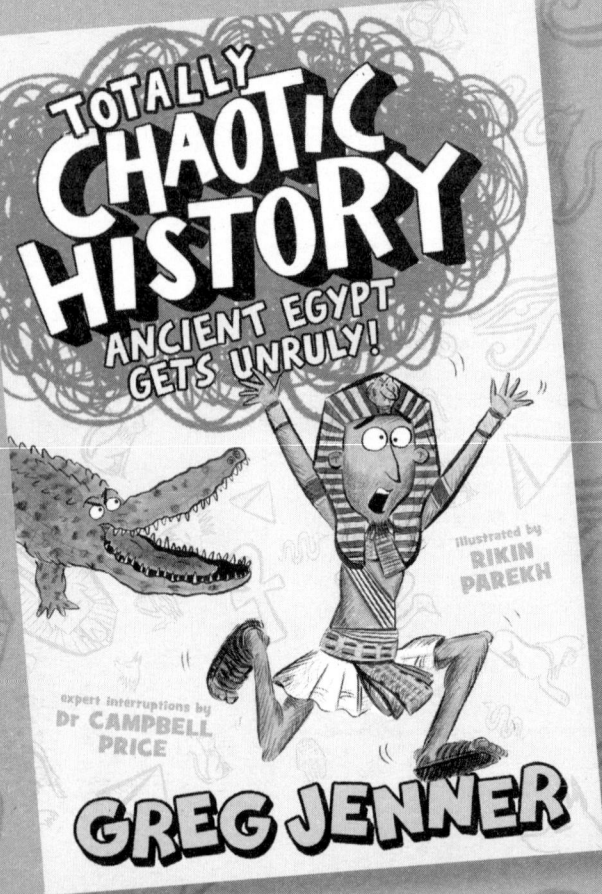

And look out for ...

Coming soon!